AFTER THE MONKEY ATE MY CHEESE

Personal Development Advice on How to Succeed in Business and in Life

Paul Georgiou

for all those who realise
we walk upon our feet
to raise our eyes
a little closer to the skies

CONTENTS

INTRODUCTION

This book gives the following guarantee:

If you follow the advice, you will succeed.

That's it. No weasel words. No qualifications. No 'Terms and Conditions' in microscopic print.

What's more, there's no gimmick, no magic trick, no silver bullet. I don't offer a hitherto undiscovered management technique, a uniquely innovative approach to problem-solving or a catchy sound bite that says it all. Nevertheless, I stand by my promise that if you follow my advice, you will succeed.

How can I be sure? I'm sure because the guarantee is based on reason and experience. Reason is available to anyone. Experience you accumulate over the years. In this book, I have looked back over the decades of my career and have distilled from that experience all the lessons I have learned.

I've made mistakes. I can help you to avoid them. (I wish someone had helped me.)

I've had success. I know how I did it, and I will tell you. That's what this book is about.

I will cover many aspects of the quest for success in business and in life, and I will illustrate the lessons with anecdotes from my own career.

Although I came from a poor family, I had the benefit of a good education (grammar school and Oxford University). But you don't need the type of education I had in order to succeed. Indeed, I now believe I would probably have progressed more quickly if I had left school at eighteen.

And you don't need to have a giant brain. If you have average (or above average) intelligence and you follow my advice, your success is assured.

Finally, to prove I mean what I say, I'm giving all the royalties from this book to charity. In the past, you must have wondered why anyone who had discovered the secret of success would ever decide to take time off from pursuing their career to write a self-help book. Surely, if they had the secret of success, they would spend their time following their own advice rather than sharing it with others. They certainly wouldn't want or need royalties from a book.

And you're right. After years of trial and error, I've followed the advice in this book and I don't want or need the royalties. So I won't take any.

On the other hand, the advice in this book is priceless and I don't want you to undervalue it. So you've had to pay for it. But all the author's royalties (10% of sales) will go to the British Red Cross. Like your success, that's guaranteed.

1

WHAT DO YOU REALLY WANT?

To see a World in a Grain of Sand
And a Heaven in a Wild flower
Hold Infinity in the palm of your hand
and Eternity in an hour.
         "Auguries of Innocence," William Blake

Let's get started. But first, you have to answer a difficult question. What is it that you really want? You might choose one or more of any number of answers. For example:

         I want to be fulfilled.
         I want to be powerful.
         I want to be rich.

Or, if you incline to altruism:

         I want to help others.
         I want to make the world a better place.
         I want to help to save the planet.

Whatever you set as your goal, the chapters in this book will help you to achieve it. Some of the advice is about progressing your career; some is simply about succeeding in life. All the advice comes from my own life experience. The lessons I teach are, in part, a record of, and a tribute to, the mistakes I've made.

First, when reading this book and answering the questions it poses, I'd ask you to be honest. We won't get anywhere if you lie. Lying is a poor basis for a relationship, especially when the relationship is with yourself.

Secondly, you have to be certain you have identified exactly what it is you want. You need to know what lies at the core of your being. And, before you decide, think deeply about your choice. I'm going to try to help you to achieve what you want, but if you don't know what you really want, my advice could be useless or, worse, counterproductive.

You may think I'm making too much of a fuss about this question – but I'm not. **Many people spend the whole of their lives pursuing something that isn't what they really want.**

The acquisitive husband who complains, when his neglected wife divorces him, "But I did it all for you" is a good example. If he did it all for his wife, clearly he was doing the wrong thing, walking the wrong path. Of course, he may be deceiving himself. He may have spent all his time at work, accumulating money, because that is truly what he wanted to do. But then he shouldn't complain when his wife leaves him because he neglected her.

Then there are others who fool themselves, forever failing to grasp or refusing to accept their own core desires. The old man, having spent decades in a job he couldn't stand, ends up with the security of his company pension, but with bitter regrets that he hasn't made more of his life.

He still doesn't fully understand that it was his choice to avoid the risk of adventure and the unknown, and that if he had a second life, he would do the same again because security means more to him than anything else.

There's another even more important reason that I put so much emphasis on this question. **The question is so important because many people never ask it.** "Why should we ask it?" they say. "Why not take life as it comes?" Well, if that's how you see things, you might as well stop reading this book now. Why? Because this book is not about taking life as it comes. Quite the opposite. It's about taking life by the scruff of the neck and, as far as possible, dragging it along the path you have chosen.

So I ask again: "What do you really want?" Take your time to answer this key question. Your choice will be the main focus of your life plan (i.e. the way in which you will achieve what you really want). Think of some of the implications of your choice. Success will certainly involve effort and probably require some sacrifice. **Proceed only if you are determined to succeed. It is truly your decision.**

1.1 YOU CAN TAKE CONTROL OF YOUR LIFE

> *It matters not how strait the gate,*
> *How charged with punishment the scroll,*
> *I am the master of my fate,*
> *I am the captain of my soul.*
> "Invictus," William Ernest Henley

Decisions! You probably think you are taking decisions all the time. You decide to get up in the morning, or you decide to lie in. You decide to go to work. You decide what clothes to wear, what breakfast to eat, what film to watch, which beer to drink.

Or do you?

There is a debate about whether we are truly making such decisions. There is evidence that many such "decisions" are taken by unconscious determinants stored in our brains and that these unconscious determinants effectively take these decisions **before** they enter our active consciousness. In other words, the impression that we are making such decisions is illusory.

There is growing evidence that most of the time our actions are determined by the way in which our brains are programmed and the recorded data they have to work on. There are now popular TV shows (e.g. C4's *Hunters*) in which ordinary people go on the run, pursued by a team of expert hunters. The fugitives try to elude capture, but the hunters investigate the lives of the fugitives and, because the fugitives tend to follow unconscious drives to act in a particular way, the hunters generally catch their prey.

That said, there's no need for us to worry about this debate because I'm talking about decisions at a higher level – decisions that are **consciously taken** after **active and often demanding mental struggle**. I'm going to differentiate these decisions from the run-of-the-mill choices we make by putting them in bold and giving them a capital **D**.

It's worth asking if you have ever taken such a **Decision**. I've been around for quite a while and I've taken very few. Here are three of them.

The first was what to read at university. At school, I studied Classics, taking Ancient Greek, Latin and Ancient History A Levels. My headmaster strongly urged me to apply to read Classics at Oxford. He insisted that my best chance of gaining a place was through Classics and certainly not through the much more competitive route of applying to read English. Against the headmaster's advice and without the benefit of any tuition (the "exigencies of the school timetable" didn't allow it), I added an A level in English to my sixth form studies and applied to New College to read English. This was a **Decision**. It was not the obvious thing to do. There were in fact strong arguments against it. But I knew I was not a natural Classicist and I felt I had an aptitude for English. So I made a **Decision**. Was it the right decision? Probably not. Not for the reason my headmaster gave – "English is not a proper subject for university study because, after all, every gentleman reads English" (it was a long time ago!) – but because I found most of the English teaching at Oxford far too vague and woolly. Now I think I should have read PPE but, at the time, I didn't know what PPE stood for.

My second **Decision** was to leave well-paid employment to set up my own consultancy business. I had been an employee for fourteen years, with a regular and ever-increasing monthly salary. I probably had another fifteen years of peak earning as an employee ahead of me. So it was a risky decision. On the other hand, I knew I would never be stretched as an employee, and I believed I could prove and fulfil myself more conclusively if I ran my own business. I accepted that I might fail. I was told that nine out of ten new businesses collapse within two years. But I knew that if I didn't try, I would regret it later. That was a **Decision**, and, as it turned out, it was a good one.

My third **Decision** was to marry my wife. I met my wife six years before I proposed. I had a feeling she was the right one for me but I valued my freedom. In the end, in a taverna on the coast road not far from the then undeveloped village of Latchi in Cyprus, on the advice of a perspicacious taverna owner, I proposed and she accepted. That was a **Decision** and, more than thirty years on, I have to say it worked out rather well.

I give a brief account of these choices I made in order to illustrate what I mean by a **Decision**. Let's try to identify the characteristics of such decisions.

Generally, a **Decision**, in the sense I use the word, is a choice between alternatives, and a choice that, to an outsider, would probably seem counterintuitive or bloody-minded. It is also often life-changing, precisely because it seems to go against the flow of one's previous life. And almost always, it involves an element of risk.

So such decisions are counterintuitive, bloody-minded, against the flow and inherently risky. Perhaps it's not surprising that many people tend to shy away from them.

That said, I'm going to argue that if you want to achieve what you really want, you will almost certainly have to take this type of decision. Why? **Because achieving what you want requires you to take control of your life.** And if you want to take control of your life, you will have to take such **Decisions**.

You will often hear people say "I had no choice."

> "*I stayed working for the company because I had no choice*" – because I wanted to protect my pension; because at my age I couldn't get another job …

> "*I stayed in this type of work because I had no choice*" – because I couldn't learn any new skills; because it's what I am …

> *"I stayed working class because I had no choice"*
> – because people like me can't do anything
> about it; because I don't have the education …

In all three cases, the individuals have reasons for staying where they are. But they *do* have a choice and they could make a **Decision** to do something about it. Such a decision may well be **counterintuitive, bloody-minded, against the flow and inherently risky**, but it's still a choice, and if you want to control your life, sometimes it's necessary to choose to decide.

There are, of course, some circumstances (e.g. disability, sickness, taxes and death) where there is no choice, but happily **for most of us, for most of our lives, we have the opportunity to make life-changing Decisions.** And **it's our fault if we choose not to make them.**

1.2 YOUR LIFE PLAN

> *Two roads diverged in a wood, and I –*
> *I took the one less traveled by.*
> "The road not taken," Robert Frost

Your life plan is the path you take from where you are today to where you want to be in the future. Your goal is to succeed in fulfilling your core objective.

Finding the path is the most difficult of the foundation tasks, especially if you seek it early in life. Why? Because when you are young, you don't have as much information as you would like on which to base your decision.

When I was young, there were vast areas of career possibilities that I didn't even consider. For example, although I had a couple of Oxford degrees, I didn't consider any of the traditional professions (e.g. accountancy, architecture, diplomacy, engineering, law or medicine). With a natural aptitude for math and having studied Classics at school and English at university, I was well prepared for a career in some of these professions; in others, I wasn't technically qualified, but I could have chosen to change direction and acquire the necessary core skills. But I didn't consider any of them. That was a shame, not because I think I should have joined one of the professions but because I unwittingly narrowed my life choices.

In passing, I should mention a conversation I had with my son and my daughter when the subject of their future careers came up. I urged them to consider the professions. By then, I had experience of using several of the professions and I said: "Consider the professions as a career. Once qualified, you can be stupid and lazy and still enjoy a standard of living well above that of the average working person." I could have expressed myself more clearly and less ambiguously. I didn't mean to suggest that all professionals were stupid and lazy. Nor was I implying that I considered my children were stupid and lazy, which is what they took me to mean and rightly reprimanded me. I simply meant that even stupid and lazy professionals (a minority, of course) could still be comfortably well-off, whereas those in other forms of employment, if stupid and lazy, could find themselves unemployed – and even if they were intelligent and industrious, they would be unlikely to earn as much as the minority of stupid and lazy members of the professions.

My advice now is that at any stage of life, keep your mind open to possibilities. Do your research. Don't be put off by any difficulties you encounter; think of what you need to do to overcome or circumvent them.

In practical terms, seek out a path that fits well with your core goal. If you really want to be rich, look for jobs where the financial rewards are great. Even if you reach the higher levels in archaeology or teaching or social work, you will not be anywhere near as well rewarded as you would be if you reached a similar level in the financial sector (banking, insurance, financial advice). So if wealth is your core goal, make sensible choices. If you consider the professions, find out the scale of rewards. For example, be aware that the average pay for engineers is well below the average pay for lawyers, despite the fact that most people (except those who determine salary levels, and lawyers) would favour engineering over the legal profession in terms of its value to society. (Today, my son is a chartered civil engineer.)

Also consider the option of setting up your own business. If successful, you will probably make more money and certainly have more control of your life than if you remain as an employee. But be aware of the risks. Most new businesses fail.

You always have to assess your chances of success if you follow a particular path. If you really want to be rich, you may be tempted by the eye-watering sums earned by top footballers. Lionel Messi and Cristiano Ronaldo both earned more than $100 million in 2018 (about $2 million a week), which puts most top bankers in the shade. But what are the chances of anyone being the world's best footballer?

If you want to make the world a better place, you have a different but no less difficult choice to make. You can either look for work in organisations that declare making the world a better place as their mission (benevolent NGOs, private charities, government departments responsible for overseas aid) or you can enter the world of politics. Broadly speaking, in the former, you will be doing your best to alleviate suffering now; in the latter, you will be trying to make the world a fairer place in the future. Both will require hard work and may well conflict with what is seen as an optimal work/life balance and high levels of remuneration – but both will at least give you a chance to achieve what you really want.

If you lean toward altruism, you might also wish to consider the caring professions (medicine, social work) as ways of fulfilling your goal.

Always focus on your goal and choose a path that at least offers the possibility of success.

1.3 THREE QUICK TIPS

I know I said "no catchy sound bites" – but what the hell!

1.3.1 "Yes, if," not "No, because"

Here's a useful tip whichever path you choose. In pursuit of your goal you will inevitably meet obstacles and challenges. Develop a mindset that always tackles such obstacles and responds to such challenges with a "Yes, if …" attitude, not a "No, because … ."

In other words, in response to any challenge, say to yourself, "**Yes**, we can do this **if** … ." Banish from your mind any response that begins, "**No**, we can't do this **because** … ."

1.3.2 Mistakes and lessons

We all make mistakes. If you have to take a decision that involves an element of risk, you'll be lucky to make the right choice half the time. But don't despair. The mistake is a perfect opportunity to learn and improve. Ask yourself: why was it the wrong choice? Could I have foreseen it was the wrong choice? Can I avoid such mistakes in future?

Turn every mistake into a lesson.

You can also learn from your successes but, in my experience, the lessons learned from mistakes are more valuable and lasting. The only real mistake is the one from which you learn nothing. And in any case, there is a downside to success – it can lead to complacency, which is a freeway to failure.

1.3.3 A real time-saver

There are some problems which you will face in life that you really can't do anything about. For example, you can't make someone love you; you can't change the past; you can't un-say what you have said; you can't change the bank rate. I could go on – the list is endless.

Although it's obvious we can't do any of these things, we have a very human tendency to worry about them, to expend a great deal of mental and emotional energy on them, energy that would be far better and more constructively spent elsewhere.

Don't! **If you can't fix it, park it**. Yes, it's difficult, but don't say you can't. Say **Yes, if …**

2

PREREQUISITES

Shame on the false Etruscan
Who lingers in his home,
When Porsena of Clusium
Is on the march for Rome.
                    "Horatius," Lord Macaulay

I'm going to lay out the prerequisites for success. These are
the qualities you will need to display if you are to succeed.
They will not, on their own, guarantee success, but if you
fail to deploy these qualities, your chances of success will be
greatly diminished.

2.1 FOCUS AND CONCENTRATION

Concentration is the secret of strength.
                    "Power," Ralph Waldo Emerson

If you want to achieve your goal, you must learn to focus all your energies on your goal and the path you have chosen to reach it. You must refuse to be diverted from the path or distracted by irrelevancies.

For some, the ability to concentrate comes easily. They understand that if you want to do your best at any task, you have to give it everything you've got. If your primary purpose is to achieve your goal, anything that dilutes your effort undermines your chances of success.

Forget multitasking. **Multitasking is simply an excuse for failing to do anything really well.** Yes, I know there is currently a tendency to admire the multitasker. And there are situations in which you have to keep your eye on several different activities at the same time. But you must accept that if you are engaged in multitasking, you will not be performing any of the tasks to the best of your ability. And believe me, if you wish to achieve your goal, you will have to work to the best of your ability.

Sadly, for many, the ability to concentrate is a lost art. It is widely accepted that the average person's attention span has dwindled to the point where anything that requires sustained mental effort is excluded from the mainstream media. This is a problem. I was listening to a BBC interview with Arthur Koestler a few years ago. I was enraged by the interviewer's compulsion to interrupt the great man long before he had finished what he had to say – so enraged that I phoned the BBC to complain. I received a courteous, well-written but brief letter a few days later which explained that BBC research had shown that the average viewer would lose interest if an interviewee took more than thirty seconds to answer a question.

More recently, I participated in a working group to discuss and define Britain's future role in a global world. The working group did a pretty good job, identifying Britain's strengths, weaknesses and opportunities and exploring various ways of exploiting the latter. It was a thorough, thought-provoking piece of work. The resulting document was well received but we were then asked to simplify it, shorten it and present the final version in a series of bullet points. God help us! Some thoughts lend themselves to such brevity; others – generally the more important, perspicacious and subtle ones – don't.

Well, the thirty-second, half-a-page-of-A4 rule may be the full extent of the attention span for the average person – but the average person is generally not successful in achieving what they want. And you're not average – at least, I hope you're not – and even if you are, you certainly won't be if you follow the advice in this book.

What can you do if you find it difficult to concentrate? First of all, don't despair. If you're young, you've been brought up in a world of sound bites, tweets of 280 characters, a world in which supposedly serious discussion programmes on TV are dominated by presenters who think they, rather than any content, are the star of the show. In other words, you've been subjected to a systematic campaign of dumbing down public and private discourse.

Even if you're older, you have lived through the last thirty years, so it's scarcely your fault if the deluge of trivia and celebrity has eroded your powers of sustained concentration.

But you can reverse the process. Start by learning a poem at least once a week. Start with a short one; then, as your memory improves, go for longer ones. Pick a subject you found difficult at school (e.g. math, geometry, English grammar), acquire a simple "teach-yourself" book and start to study it. Take one step at a time and try as hard as you can to grasp each module fully. **Get your head down, put your fingers in your ears and concentrate.**

It sounds easy but it won't be. For a generation that spends half its life listening to ear-splitting music on earphones and the other half selecting emojis on their mobiles, the experience of really concentrating on a complex subject could well be truly novel. But keep at it. As you take ownership of the poems and begin to grasp a subject you found difficult at school, you will regain your self-confidence and your self-respect. Instead of allowing the unending stream of drivel briefly to occupy your mind before it is flushed away almost immediately by the next surge of inanity, you will, at the very least, have taken possession of content that endures, mental input that contains considered and worthwhile thoughts, subjects that help you to understand some aspect of reality.

Why undertake such exercises? Because you will need to focus and concentrate if you are to implement your life plan – and a little gentle exercise of your memory and your analytical faculties will help you to succeed. (More on this later.)

If you would like a selection of short and medium length poems to get you started, see Appendix A.

2.2 DETERMINATION

If you can force your heart and nerve and sinew
To serve your turn long after they are gone,
And so hold on when there is nothing in you
Except the Will which says to them: "Hold on!"
"If," Rudyard Kipling

There's another quality you will need to apply – determination. Don't give up. Whatever life throws at you, whatever setbacks you face, just pick yourself up and keep going. **Determination is not the key to success; but it is a prerequisite**. The seemingly laid-back Irish singer Val Doonican jokingly declared it had taken him "seventeen years to become an overnight success." Seventeen years may be excessive, but behind every really successful person there are hours, days, weeks and years of hard work.

You can't always win, but the moment you give up you lose. I learned a useful lesson when I was eleven. My school encouraged those who were interested to learn how to box. One day I was put into a boxing match with a boy called Francis Denham. We were of roughly equal height, weight and boxing expertise, which is why we were matched. We went at it for three rounds, doing as much damage to each other as two eleven-year-old boys wearing boxing gloves can do. It was a hard fight. Toward the end of the third round I remember thinking: "If he hits my face one more time, I am going to have to quit." Exhausted, I managed to throw one last punch. The punch was no harder than any of those he or I had landed before. It was at this point that Francis started to cry. Evidently both of us had reached the end of our tethers. He had felt what I had felt – but I had thrown what was to be the final punch. It was just one more punch than he could throw. Suddenly, from facing defeat I became the victor. All the pain disappeared. I generously consoled my battered opponent.

I'm sure – at least, I hope – that Francis soon forgot the fight. But I remember it still, decades later, not because I won but because it taught me an important life lesson. **The difference between success and failure is often much**

less than we imagine – just one more punch, just one more try. Success is often determined simply by who tries harder, who persists longer. **You never know when you are going to win – so you just have to keep trying until you find out.**

2.3 WORKING HARD

Sheer plod makes plough down sillion shine.
"The Windhover," Gerard Manley Hopkins

There's one other precondition of success in achieving your goal. Hard work! Sorry, but it's true. Natural ability helps but any successful individual, whether they are an administrator, an artist, a businessman, an electrician, a footballer, a plumber, a politician, a teacher, or, indeed, anything else, will have worked very hard to achieve excellence and the rewards that go with it. **Those with less talent can succeed with hard work; those with more talent will fail without it.** As they say, the only place where success comes before work is in a dictionary.

As with "taking a decision" we have to define what we mean by "hard work." Many people claim to work hard. Most of them are lying – at least, in the sense I am using the term here.

When I was at school and university, I took temporary jobs during most vacations. I worked as a factory worker (packing straw into test tubes and test tubes into straw), a market researcher (investigating the viability of containerisation), a postman (loading and unloading Braille books for blind people on and off freight trains through the night), painter (painting, among many other things, the toilets at Harrow public school), a sports ground attendant (where I inadvertently ran the gang mowers over a beautifully prepared cricket pitch), a security guard (taking the payroll to Cowley Motor Works), and a waiter in the Tudor Restaurant just off Leicester Square (where, aged fifteen, returning home at midnight, I successfully declined the blandishments of the hookers on my way to the Tube).

I learned a great deal from these experiences, but what struck me most was the disinclination of most people to work hard, even when there were financial incentives to put in the effort.

At the factory, I was asked by the foreman one day, as an emergency measure, to abandon my test-tube packing duties and take over the Goods Inwards department. The two men who ran the department were both unavailable for work (one was abroad on holiday; the other was off sick).

"It's just for a couple of days," said the foreman. "Hold the fort as best you can. I'll get someone experienced to help you as soon as possible."

I remained alone in charge of the Goods Inwards department for four weeks. Even if you stretched it out, there was no more than two hours work a day for one person. When the time came for me to leave, the foreman called me into his office. He said: "I know you're studying and going off to college, so you probably won't be interested, but if you ever want a job, come and see me."

Working for the Post Office (which I did several times at Christmas) was particularly enlightening. I always worked the night shift. My main job was loading and unloading sacks containing books for blind people. I have no idea what the books for blind people looked like but I know they were heavy.

"Don't make too much noise when loading the sacks," said the postman in charge of the temporary labour.

"Why's that?" I asked. It seemed an odd instruction as the sacks were heavy and made a noise when you loaded them.

"The permanent staff are sleeping in that room and they don't like to be disturbed."

It turned out that the "permanent staff" were clocking up extraordinary levels of overtime, at double normal rates, by sleeping on the premises overnight and then getting up to do their day shift.

On my first job as a painter-decorator, I was tasked with painting the railings that enclosed the land on which Hendon Magistrates Court stood. The rest of the team were fulfilling the important part of the contract – painting the outside of the building itself. The foreman, a young man with ambition, incentivised by promise of a bonus if he could complete the job ahead of schedule, decided to cut a few corners. Instead of sanding down, priming, applying one undercoat and two top coats, he decided to dispense with the sanding, priming and undercoating, going straight to the application of the top coat. After several days, when I was only half way through the painting of the railings (there were a lot of them), a works inspector paid us a visit, realised what was happening, and threw us all off the site.

As security guard, my first job was to guard the fully stocked M&S store in Oxford throughout one night. For some reason one of the external walls was missing and had been temporarily replaced by an enormous canvas sheet, leaving it open to anyone who wanted to engage in a nocturnal shopping spree. (Happily, no one did.) My regular role was to sit in the back of the armoured van with the cash that had to be delivered safely to clients. I was locked in the back and only I could open the door.

"What do I do if we're attacked?" I asked.

"Open the door," I was told. "We're not going to take any risks for the kind of money we're paid."

I was given a dye gun. As a joke, I asked: "What do I do with this? Point it at the robbers and say 'Die'?"

It didn't even raise a smile. It was gently explained to me that if we were attacked, I should use it to spray the money with an indelible ink.

The job I did most regularly was waiting. The father of one of my school friends ran a restaurant in Rupert Street, just off Leicester Square. From the age of fifteen I worked in the Tudor Restaurant most holidays until I went up to Oxford. I worked twelve hours a day, six days a week and earned as much as the average working man at that time. The pay was poor. The key to earning that level of remuneration was tips. From the moment a customer entered till the moment they left, I had only one thought: "How big a tip can I earn?" I was a good waiter. I realised there was no guarantee of a tip. The Tudor Restaurant was really a café which offered good but cheap fare for visitors to London – not the best establishment for winning impressive tips. But if you looked after the customers, paid attention to them when they wanted service, and dealt with their needs efficiently and quickly, most could be induced to leave you something. My best tip was provided by two American ladies who left me a tip equal to fifty percent of their bill. My co-worker was Don, an alcoholic in his forties. He was a competent waiter who did as much as, but no more than, was required. Although vastly more experienced, he accumulated fewer tips than me.

On every job I took, I was stunned by the disinclination of most people to work hard or, in some cases, to work at all. When I recount these experiences, I'm sometimes told that that was "back in the day." I'm assured that "things are very different now."

Fair enough. Let's consider work as it is today – and what "hard work" really means.

Let's first of all exclude from the "hardworking" category most office workers. It has been estimated that UK office workers spend anything up to two hours of the working day (i.e. just under 30%) on social media or shopping sites and on matters unrelated to their work. Even if we think this is an exaggeration, and we say the average is one hour a day, that's still 15% of the working day. Given the reticence of respondents in answering questions about their time-wasting activities at work, 30% is, in fact, likely to be an underestimate, rather than an overestimate. If we add the time spent by the convivial and garrulous British worker chatting with workmates, we are probably not far off downtime amounting to 50% of the working day. Hence, perhaps, Britain's notoriously poor productivity figures.

Many white-collar workers work long hours, but they spend much of their time at meetings – and travelling to and from them. Meetings that are well run, have a clear purpose and a precisely defined agenda, that are attended by articulate, coherent participants and presided over by an expert chairman who ensures that every action required is allocated to someone present who will be held accountable for implementing it can be really useful. But they're not the type of meetings *you* attend, now are they?

What's more, when I use the term "hard work," I mean much more than putting in "a fair day's work for a fair day's pay." To begin to define hard work in the sense that I mean it, we had best look at those who succeed in setting up a business from scratch.

Generally speaking, all normal measurements of hard work have to be recalibrated. Such people don't work eight hours a day; they work ten, twelve or more hours a day. They spend all their waking hours thinking about their business; how to improve their product or service; how to recruit and train staff; how to finance their fledgling business in the early years, and later, how to win and hold customers; how to fight the competition; and, of course, how to get the work itself done. And all this while taking far less money out of the business than they could easily earn as an employee and knowing throughout that there is no safety net if things go wrong.

I know what I'm talking about. In my late thirties, after fourteen years as an employee, I set up my own business. At the time, I was working for Visnews (now Reuters TV), then the world's leading television news agency (owned by the BBC, Reuters and the Australian, Canadian and New Zealand broadcasting corporations). While at Visnews I'd had an idea for a new service. I tried to sell the idea to Visnews but the company was unconvinced of the concept's potential.

So I set up my own company in December 1978. A year later, I resigned from Visnews and, on January 1st, 1980, I started to work for my own company. (This, you will recall, was the second of my **Decisions**.) I was sure my idea – for the formal analysis of the content, reach and effect of media coverage on governments and companies – could work. Cheap computer processing power was essential to my idea. Happily, personal computers were just becoming available at affordable prices.

In the first few years, it looked as though Visnews' scepticism about the potential of media coverage analysis was justified. I talked to government ministries and companies. There was interest but no buyers. I supported myself with consultancy work and freelance market research and marketing projects, but I continued to promote the merits of my idea at every opportunity.

Toward the end of this initial period, I married my wife (my third **Decision**).

Then after five years, I persuaded the Ministry of Information in Saudi Arabia to buy the service for one year (1985). The contract involved taking apart coverage of Saudi Arabia in the British and American media, identifying each news story, the audience it reached and the likely effect of the coverage on the audience. Each article was coded for news story, topic and messages, with an "audience reached"

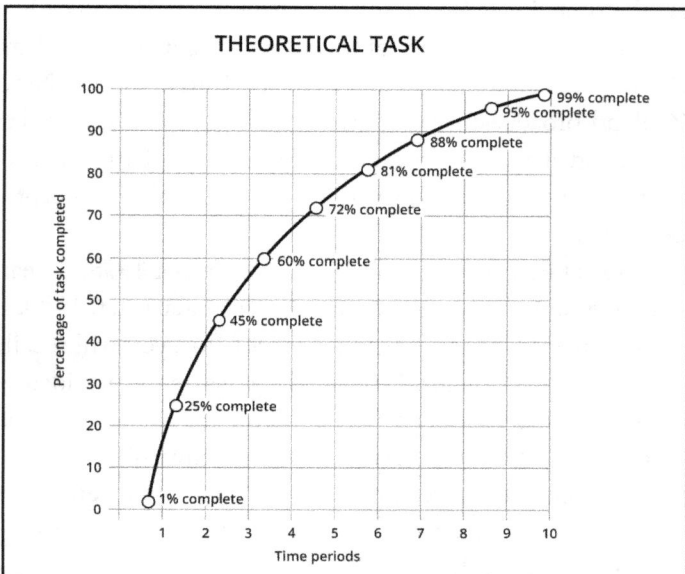

THEORETICAL TASK

Percentage of task completed

1% complete
25% complete
45% complete
60% complete
72% complete
81% complete
88% complete
95% complete
99% complete

Time periods

figure and an assessment of the effect. We then produced a report, with editorial comment and illustrated with charts, on the impact of the coverage on the image of Saudi Arabia in the West. (As it turned out, the contract was renewed for twenty years and provided the foundation for my company, Panarc International.)

For three years, we had no competitors. We added client after client in the Middle East, and then later almost every UK government department, all sections of the BBC (national and regional), BT and many major financial, commercial and charitable organisations.

From the start and from then on, it was hard work. I regularly worked from 9 a.m. to midnight, six or seven days a week, analysing the data, writing reports and improving MAX, our own computer program, with Stephen Arnold, my programmer. **It was hard work in the sense that I mean it**.

After three years, competitors arrived. We held our own because the computer program we had developed for the analysis was far more sophisticated than theirs, but as time passed they improved and redirected the service away from the boards of companies (our original target market) toward the public relations departments within them. Media coverage analysis (today generally called media evaluation) is now a small but substantial industry with a dozen or so companies operating in the UK and dozens more in countries around the world.

I recount my experience simply to assure you that my advice is not purely theoretical; it is based on personal experience. It comes not from a business school but from life. And I tell you a bit of my story not to claim any particular talent, but to illustrate what can be achieved if you are single-minded, determined and **hardworking**. Someone said

"Genius is 10% inspiration and 90% perspiration." I don't know about genius, but **success is 10% inspiration, 20% concentration, 30% determination and 40% hard work.**

I hope I haven't put you off. Quite reasonably some, perhaps many, might think that this is all too much. They might well say: "If achieving success involves that amount of commitment and effort, it's not for me." Fair enough. After all, although almost everyone can succeed, most don't – and they don't succeed precisely because they aren't prepared to give it that amount of commitment and effort. If you are one such, I still hope you will carry on reading simply out of interest to see how those who follow my advice can optimise their chances of success. You never know, you might change your mind and rejoin the journey!

If you are not deterred, if you are still with me, I want to make a final point in this section. You will notice that at no point have I suggested that you need to be particularly clever. **Nowhere have I said that being very bright, intellectually accomplished, in possession of an outstanding IQ, is a requirement for success. Because it isn't.** If you have average intelligence or above, are focused, determined and work hard, you will succeed. Indeed, being very clever can be an impediment. You need common sense, a faculty that is sometimes denied those who are intellectually gifted. And in business, you need to understand your customers, an ability often beyond those who have dwelt too long in the sylvan groves of Academe.

So let's move on.

2.3.1 Work/Life balance

The suggestion that people should work hard faces several serious objections in today's world. The most serious of these objections is expressed in the concept of the work/life balance.

The concept is interesting because it separates work from life. There is *working*, and then there is *living*. It implies that work somehow has a tendency to encroach on life and has to be put back in its place.

It's a false dichotomy. Work is part of life. Indeed, for most of us for most of our lives it is what we spend much of our time doing. **I think it's fair to say that the concept of work/life balance is a rhetorical trick to strengthen the argument that work should be downgraded in importance to allow "life" to flourish.**

The real dichotomy is work/leisure balance or, in economic terms, the balance between earning the money and spending it. Of course, there are also the relationships with family and friends, but these relationships – and the leisure time in which to enjoy them – are made possible by your work, and are supported and sustained by the money you earn. Viewed in these terms, work regains the respect and status it deserves. If you see work as a necessary evil that unfairly competes with what really matters, you will not be a success.

And the good sense of balancing work and leisure, as two important constituents of life, is perfectly exemplified in the running of a home. Running a home and rearing children is one of the most important of all undertakings, and as anyone knows who has done it, success (i.e. doing it well and balancing work and leisure in the family) requires all the skills covered in this book – and, of course, long hours of unremitting hard work. Your objective is success. Whatever your goal, hard work is a precondition.

But there's something else. Work gives people a sense of self-worth, a sense of purpose, and a framework for life that helps to give life meaning. We can't all find satisfying, exciting, creative, challenging, and fulfilling jobs, but even the dull, repetitive, boring work that many have to do still gives shape and purpose to lives that might well otherwise degenerate into apathy and chaos. Hard work – and the satisfaction (and often the success) that rewards it – can be a powerful antidote to mental and physical disability. We abandon the idea of work as an essential, valuable, and beneficial element of life at our peril.

There will be those who argue that we should look forward to a world run by artificial intelligence (AI), relieving mankind of the burden of work. AI will surely change our world, and I guess no one will miss boring, repetitive jobs and types of work that involve anti-social hours or conditions. But we had better find other constructive work for people if they are to retain their self-respect and sense of purpose. Otherwise, I'm pretty sure society will be overwhelmed by a plague of mental illnesses and dysfunctional relationships.

"Surely many would welcome a life without work?" you ask. "Didn't you say many people are inherently lazy?" Yes. I said that there is a tendency in many to idleness – but not as a full-time occupation.

2.4 BETTERING

You never know what is enough until you know what is more than enough.
"Proverbs of Hell," William Blake

I thought of calling this section "Perfectionism." But then I changed my mind. Perfectionism is the pursuit of the perfect, and since we can never achieve perfection, I would be setting an unattainable goal. I then considered calling the section "Amelioration." But then I thought the word was not quite right. Amelioration is about making bad things better, and what I mean is continually striving, not just to make the bad good but to make the good excellent. So I decided on "Bettering" (i.e. the habit of making things better). **Whatever you do, cultivate the habit of constructive dissatisfaction and self-criticism**. How could I have done better? Is there a better way of doing this?

It's extraordinary how we can put up with something that doesn't work well, that irritates us, but about which we never bother to do anything. For years, my wife and I used sponges for washing up. When the sponge became past its best, it was relegated to the task of washing the dogs' bowls. Not infrequently we would muddle up our washing-up sponge with the dog-bowl sponge. It wasn't a catastrophe, but it wasn't what we intended. This minor irritation went on for years until we hit on the idea of nipping the corner off any washing-up sponge which was to be demoted to dog-bowl cleaning. From that day, there was never a mix-up. It didn't change the world but it does provide a simple example of the benefits of always asking "Is there a better way?"

I've never written anything that I couldn't improve on a second reading – and generally on a third and fourth as well. Saying exactly what you mean, so that it encapsulates what you want to say with elegance and economy, so that it cannot possibly mean anything else, has become a rare accomplishment. Several edits may be necessary to get close to such clarity.

When I was running my media coverage analysis business, I worked closely with my programmer, Stephen Arnold, for twenty-five years. Throughout that time, we developed and refined the program that performed the analysis. There was literally no end to the improvements we could make.

In other words, **acquire the habit of self-criticism to ensure you are being and doing the best you can.**

That said, there has to be a qualification. In most, if not all, activities, there comes a point when the reward for further effort is not sufficient to justify the effort. It's the law of diminishing returns. Cleaning a house is a good example. If you spend an hour cleaning a house, at the end of the hour it will be cleaner than it was but it will be far from clean. If you spend two hours, at the end of two hours, it will be almost twice as clean as it was after one hour. But if you clean it for 10 hours, that last hour will make only a very small, perhaps imperceptible, improvement. (See the chart below.)

Depending on the standard you set (or the value you put on your time), there will be a point when you decide that further effort is no longer justified by the diminishing improvement you will achieve.

In the chart below, it will be obvious that the theoretical task is half completed in a little under three time periods. It will take another seven periods to reach 99% perfection. If you have to work under pressure, the ability to judge when that optimum point has been reached is a major asset. (See 5.1.1 The urgent v. the important, for further comment.)

How do you calculate the optimum?

There is no fixed rule. Everything depends on the standard you set and the other demands on your time.

Of even more value is the ability to achieve the best possible result within the time available.

Let's say, in our theoretical example, you have only three time periods to allocate to the task. You could decide that you will simply complete half the job (not a good idea unless you plan to allocate more time on another occasion to finish it!). The trick in this situation is to understand how long you have got and then to complete the whole of the task, **as best you can,** in the allotted time.

When I was at school, one of the key exercises we had to perform was the précis. We were given an article of 1,000 words and asked to summarise it, covering the main points, in 250 words; and then again into 100 words. The exercise forces you to analyse the content of the article and to hierarchise the points made.

That's what's required here. **You need to précis tasks, just as you précis articles.** If there isn't time to perform the whole task to 99% perfection, then précis the task and **perform the key elements of the whole task to the highest level you can in the time available.** Of course, the work won't be as well done as it would be if you had more time – but the task is completed as well as it could be, given the time constraints.

Some people find this easy; many people don't. If you can master this technique (because you have a natural aptitude or acquire it through practice), you will have a major advantage over those who can't. (See also 5.2 Quality v. Speed, and 5.2.2 The perfect v. the good)

3

LUCK

Diligence is the mother of good fortune.
Miguel de Cervantes

"What about luck?" I hear you ask. "Why haven't you included luck in your formula for success? Many of the most successful people seem to have been blessed. Some were born lucky. Some just happened to be in the right place at the right time. Surely luck is crucial."

It's a fair question. Everyone needs a bit of luck. And some people are definitely unlucky (e.g. if you lose your good health, or if you are handicapped in some way). Accidents can set us back. Catastrophes can happen.

And yes, others are lucky. If you win $100 million in a lottery, that's luck.

But being lucky is not the same as being successful. And this book is about success. The man who wins $100 million is not a success. He's lucky and he's rich. But his win does not make him a success. Success is achieving your goal through your own efforts.

Very often we confuse luck (which we can't control) with the ability to recognise and take opportunities. We all have opportunities. We can all study or train to acquire a new skill. We can all practice to develop and refine a talent we have. In our careers, we can apply for a promotion or seek to change employers at any time there is a vacancy.

These are all opportunities. If we seize them, others may say we were lucky. You could call it that. If we ignore them, we may feel we are unlucky. But that isn't fair. If you seize an opportunity, that's a good decision. If you ignore it, you can't blame anyone but yourself.

To be "lucky", you just need to be open to possibilities and opportunities.

When I first set up my own business, I survived on freelance consultancy work for the first few years. At Visnews I had spent years marketing films in the Middle East (mainly Saudi Arabia), so I was able to offer research and consultancy services in the Saudi market. I could help companies to navigate their way through the Saudi regulations and bureaucratic procedures.

But wait a minute. If I could help other companies to market their products and services, surely I could do the same for myself. All I needed was a product.

Before working for Visnews I had spent seven years in market research and marketing, working for major Swiss pharmaceutical company. In those years I had developed an interest in, and some understanding of, the drug and health-food market.

I had always been interested in royal jelly since reading the Roald Dahl story of that name, so when I heard, by chance, of a company marketing fresh royal jelly as a miraculous health food, I was intrigued. I became even more intrigued when I learned that the company making the product was eager to expand its business in overseas markets. I arranged to meet Irene, the owner of the company, an attractive Jewish lady. We got on well at once. We seemed to have the same attitude to business and the same ability to grasp immediately the structure and dynamics of a deal. Her main product was fresh royal jelly in capsule form. She sold it in packs of thirty capsules. When I mentioned my particular expertise in dealing with the Saudi market, she immediately conceded that, for obvious reasons, the Saudi market was not one she could approach. After all, she was a woman and a Jew. I said I could help to market her product in Saudi Arabia and other parts of the Arab world. I asked her for her best wholesale price for a pack of thirty capsules. She said it was £4. I said I would sell each pack for £6, so I would want one third commission on all sales that I arranged. She said that if I could sell packs for £6 each, it was fine by her. We drew up an agreement and I was appointed the company's agent for the Arab Middle East.

On my next trip to Saudi Arabia, I introduced Samir, a Palestinian friend, to royal jelly. He asked me what was so special about the substance and how did I justify the price. I gave him the facts about the constituents and about the medical evidence for its efficacy. I mentioned the 3% of fresh royal jelly that has so far defied analysis. But I said that the key constituent, in common with all health foods, was hope. "And who," I asked, "can put a price on that?"

Samir was an astute businessman who knew how to work a deal. He agreed that for one third of what I earned on sales of the product, he would undertake to sell the product in the Kingdom and introduce me to the owners of health-food outlets in other parts of the Arabian Gulf.

The enterprise was surprisingly successful. With Samir's encouragement, customers for the product became convinced of royal jelly's capacity to increase virility. I thought this a little odd, given that the amazing effects of royal jelly centred on the female bee which, by ingesting the substance, becomes bigger, lives longer and gives birth to vast numbers of other bees. But whatever the customers thought royal jelly could do, they bought it. We got small orders; then we got larger orders. Our telex machine (it was a long time ago) in my office in Ealing shuddered into life, and there was another order worth £60,000. Our take on that order was £20,000. We passed the order and shipping instructions to Irene, and invoiced her as soon as the purchaser advised us the money had been paid.

Why do I recount this particular venture? Because I hope it illustrates the points I am making about:

(a) being open to possibilities

(b) seizing opportunities

I was primarily interested in launching my concept of media coverage analysis, but while waiting for my first sale of the service (it was a five-year wait!), I had to support myself. I undertook market research and consultancy assignments in the UK. This work enabled me to survive. But I asked myself whether I had any particular asset that might offer additional opportunities. Yes, I had some years of experience working the Saudi market and had made good contacts. So I was on the lookout for another way of earning money.

You could say I was lucky to hear of Irene and her royal jelly company; that I was lucky she was both Jewish and a female, which precluded her from approaching a large market with which I was particularly familiar; that I was lucky she and I hit it off; that I was lucky I had a contact in Saudi Arabia who could see the potential of the business.

On the other hand, I would argue that I was simply following the advice I am giving in this book. I decided what I needed to do (open up a new revenue stream), looked around for possibilities, adopted a "Yes, if …" attitude, and focused all my energies on setting up the business.

I will concede one point to luck. In this instance, I was not personally required to work particularly hard. But none of the rewards would have come unless I had seized the opportunity. Carpe diem, for sure; carpe potestatum ("seize the opportunity") even more so.

4

CORE ABILITIES

Men at some time are master of their fates;
The fault, dear Brutus, is not in our stars,
But in ourselves, that we are underlings.

Julius Caesar, William Shakespeare

What are the abilities that will bring you success? In essence, they are the ability to think and the ability to feel. The good news is that, to some degree at least, we all possess these abilities. The even better news is that if these abilities have not so far been fully developed, they can be refined and enhanced by exercise and application.

4.1 REASONING

Reason obeys itself; and Ignorance submits to
whatever is dictated to it.

The Rights of Man, Thomas Paine

Please don't be offended but I have to ask: do you value reason? By that I mean are you at home with the idea of consistency, of logical connections, of rational discourse.

Why do I ask? I ask because:

(1) many people no longer value reason, or they see it as a relatively unimportant way of looking at things

(2) all my advice depends on acceptance of the primacy of reason

Let's take these points one at a time and justify them.

(1) many people no longer value reason, or they see it as a relatively unimportant way of looking at things

We now live in a world in which rational discourse has been very much downgraded in the hierarchy of modes of communication. Hypersensitivity to others' feelings and the rights of others to elevate their feelings above reason are much in vogue.

It's no longer acceptable to make incontrovertibly true statements of fact if they are offensive to one of the many communities and constituencies in modern society. What's more, even if your remarks are not offensive by any objective criteria, if they are felt to be offensive by anyone, then, according to current thinking, those remarks will be judged offensive and you will be considered guilty of giving offence. This is now the law.

It is creating (or consolidating) what is rather quaintly but unkindly called the snowflake generation. In considering many issues, it is now no longer permissible to express perfectly rational arguments or objective observations of reality. For many people now, the key determinant in deciding which argument or policy is persuasive is not whether it is rational or consistent but simply whether or not they feel comfortable with it. Many people today will:

- vote for a reduction in taxes while demanding higher investment in public services
- enthusiastically support abortion but balk at executing serial murderers
- express horror at the accidental death of an individual killed in a traffic accident while happily supporting military adventures that kill tens or hundreds of thousands of innocent civilians
- do as little as possible for the money they are paid and still expect their employer to thrive
- pay their employees as little as possible for the work they do and still expect their employees to remain highly motivated.

There are many good reasons for some of this re-engineering of mental reality, for ignoring glaring inconsistencies in moral judgements, for insisting that things are not as they are. It is a good way of silencing bigots of various types. And it can provide or restore self-esteem to those in society who have traditionally been undervalued. So I accept that, in general discourse, there are justifications for this approach to thought and language (widely, although in my view incorrectly, called political correctness).

But if you are entirely comfortable with this more emotional, less rational, mode of thinking, if you disrespect the discipline of rational thought, you may have a bit of a problem with some of the subsequent sections in this book because of the problem identified in (2) below.

(2) all my advice depends on acceptance of the primacy of reason

Of course I acknowledge that there are many factors that affect and impinge upon our mental processes (and I'm not for a moment underestimating the value of empathy, see Section 4.5), but the secure foundation for thought is reason. So once again, I have to ask: "Are you with me?"

Do you like to base your thinking and your decisions on reasoned argument? Do you feel uncomfortable if you find yourself holding contradictory views on a particular subject? If your answer is "Yes" to both these questions, then we will get along fine. What I advise, based on experience and reason, will make sense to you.

If you are less enthusiastic about reason and incline to a less analytical, more temperamental view of life, if you feel comfortable with incoherent argument, permeated with inconsistencies, fair enough. Please continue reading – but you may find some of the subsequent sections grate a little on your sensibilities.

4.2 THE ORGANISING MIND

> *Organising is what you do before you do something, so that when you do it, it is not all mixed up.*
>
> *Winnie the Pooh*, A. A. Milne

I include this section on the organising mind with mixed feelings.

In its favour, it encapsulates the mental disciplines I have applied to every task I have undertaken and it has proved its worth to me a thousand times. These disciplines have enabled me to bring order out of chaos, to make sense of raw data, to impose structure on, and discern, solutions to many of life's problems.

Against it, I admit it is out of tune with current educational theory and the zeitgeist of today.

So you make up your own mind. If, after reading the rest of this introduction, you think it might be helpful, read on. If you're not interested, skip to 4.3 Communicating.

oooOooo

This is what I think. If you are going to be focused, determined, and industrious, you will need to be organised. You may well be a natural organiser. I suspect that if you have leapt the hurdles I have put in your way so far and reached this point, then you have a natural aptitude for imposing order on chaos. But read on. Some of what I have to say might still be useful.

I realised very early in life that there are some simple techniques for "sorting things out." These techniques are as relevant to preparing a shopping list as they are to devising a structure for a personal development book or handling the most complex project. They are:

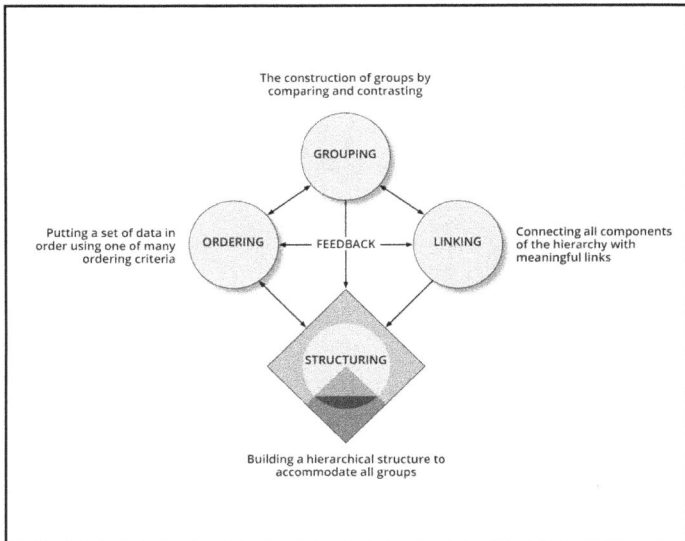

Back in the day, these simple techniques were taught in primary school. Today, it seems they are largely ignored. But they are essential if we are to grasp and understand the unending flow of data about which so many in business are forever complaining. They are the techniques that enable us **to make data make sense.**

Some of you will be asking why I devote so much space in a book on how to succeed in business and in life to the simplest and most elementary of mental activities. I have three reasons:

(1) There are now many people who are unfamiliar with these techniques and, even if they are aware of them, have not been taught to employ them routinely in performing tasks.

(2) To succeed in implementing your life plan, you will need to use your time well. Anything that can help you to perform efficiently is of very real value.

(3) I have used these techniques throughout my life – in school (to pass exams); in university (to earn degrees); and in business (to negotiate deals, to draw up contracts, and to implement projects) – and they have served me well, as I believe they will serve you well if you employ them.

4.2.1 Grouping

Grouping is a fundamental skill that enables us to comprehend and manage large quantities of information which, at first sight, might seem formless or chaotic. It provides the basis for structuring (the fourth technique).

For many people in business, the ability to group data is second nature. Nevertheless, it is still worth setting out some basic rules. And it may furnish some useful guidelines on how to grasp, order and, indeed, add meaning to those floods of information by which we are all inundated.

We should perhaps emphasise the adding of meaning. In any set of data, there is of course meaning in each of the units that make up the set, but grouping allows you to add meaning simply by the act of grouping. Grouping tells the reader the criterion the grouper is applying in order to construct the group. That criterion is itself an additional unit of meaning.

How do we constitute groups? We **compare and contrast**. We look for characteristics or features that items have in common and that are not shared by other items.

At its simplest, the compare-and-contrast technique enables us to divide things into groups on the basis of physical characteristics, e.g. size, weight, shape. At a more sophisticated level we can analyse data on populations by gender, social class, political affiliations, etc. And at the highest level, we can compare and contrast ideas and arguments, identifying features of each so that we can see similarities and differences, and links within each group. This technique is particularly useful when marshalling arguments in preparation for negotiations. (For an example of grouping ideas, see Appendix B, Grouping.)

4.2.2 Ordering

This is all about putting things in order. There are various criteria you can use:

- alphabetical (a neutral form of ranking in that it adds no meaning to the data ordered)
- causal (showing the causal relationship between the data, if there is one)
- chronological (showing the temporal sequence of the data, e.g. earliest first)

- general to particular (showing the parent of a group and then its children and grandchildren, etc.)
- ranking (showing the data in order of importance)

The application of these ordering criteria is useful when preparing documents of all types.

I find it extraordinary that, in so many documents, the significance and value of ordering is ignored. Lists appear, not in alphabetical order (a neutral order), not in order of importance or priority, or time sequence or any other criterion, but in random order.

This is a mistake. First, an opportunity to add meaning to the list has been lost; secondly, the reader may assume there is a significance in the order that is not intended. After all, man is a meaning-seeking creature. Order is a means of communicating *your* meaning.

Ranking is particularly useful in ordering lists of tasks to determine the sequence in which they should be performed (see 5.1.2 Lists).

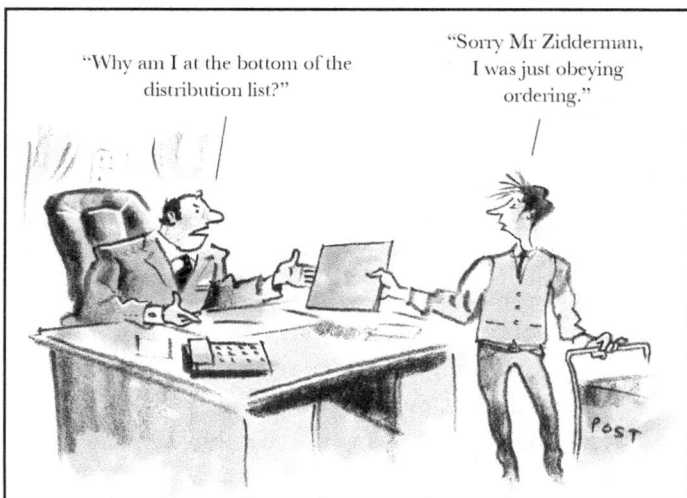

"Why am I at the bottom of the distribution list?"

"Sorry Mr Zidderman, I was just obeying ordering."

4.2.3 Linking

Here is a list of nine types of link (the way in which we connect bits of information together in order to make sense of them). When thinking, speaking or writing, using the right link to join your thoughts together is a crucial skill.

Types of link	Some verbal link indicators
causal	because
combining	and
consequential	consequently, so that, therefore
contrasting	but, on the other hand, in contrast
conditional	if, on condition that, with the prerequisite, with the precondition, when
elucidating	thus
exceptional	despite, except
purposive	in order to, to
temporal	subsequently, then, when, whereupon

The verbal indicators can be adjectives, adverbs, prepositions or conjunctions. They serve to indicate the connection between bits of information.

Using the right link makes clear the nature of the connection between two elements of data. Correct linking is essential in presenting arguments, preparing documents and in intelligent conversation.

In practice, correct linking also helps to ensure operations are performed as efficiently as possible.

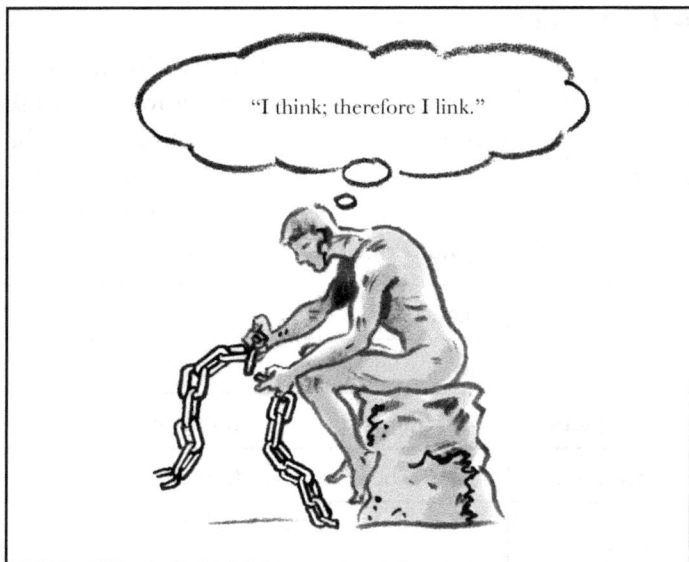

4.2.4 Structuring

Structuring means the arrangement (usually in hierarchical form) of a set of information in a graded order that shows the relationship between all the parts which make up the set and that adds meaning to the set by virtue of the principles on which the hierarchy is formed. (In preparing a structure, you use the techniques of grouping, ordering and linking.)

A Table of Contents is a good example of a structure for a book. A Critical Path Analysis is a good example of a structure for a project. Such structures are generally hierarchical, based on principles of:

- causality
- general to the particular
- relative importance
- temporal sequence

or any combination of these four.

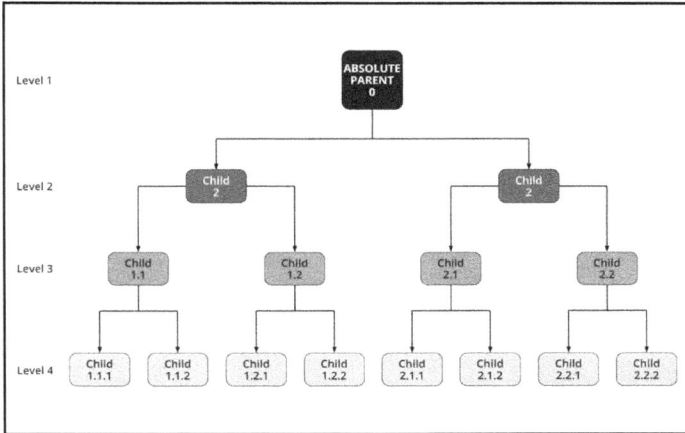

4.2.5 Conclusion

There is a way of thinking that underlies this section on the organising mind. The techniques listed here are all about imposing order on disorder.

The habitual use of these techniques will have a number of beneficial effects. It will keep your mind sharp; it will improve your communication skills; it will help you to achieve clarity in your planning and efficiency in the execution of your plan.

There is no part of life – whether you are shopping in a supermarket, planning a party, managing a business project, preparing a report, arguing a case, negotiating a contract or working out your life plan – that will not benefit from the application of these techniques.

Author's Note: For those who are interested, read my *Report Writer's Handbook*, which explores in detail the principles and benefits of grouping, ordering, linking and structuring. (For further details or to order, go to the Panarc Publishing website: www.panarcpublishing.com.)

I have also devised a computer program, **DocuPraxis®**, which is a project management and document preparation application. Further information and licences are available for purchase at www.docupraxis.co.uk.

4.3 COMMUNICATING

What oft was thought, but ne'er so well expressed
An Essay on Criticism, Alexander Pope

As noted before, to ensure success in the goals you have set, you will need to apply some core abilities. Once again, they are abilities that either you already possess or which, with effort and application, you can acquire. I include in this section some didactic elements that may grate with many readers. I apologise, but I need to set out the skills you need to succeed and I think it best to be blunt. Let me explain.

Modern educational practice has brought many improvements to our teaching system. It has, for example, widened the syllabus, and challenged children to expand their horizons and question received wisdom. But there have been some negatives. Some of the basic educational skills have suffered.

I have recruited graduates (even one or two from Oxbridge) who have had only a very shaky grasp of English grammar, who have found it difficult to express their meaning precisely and concisely, who are flummoxed by percentages, and who can be easily misled by statistics. This should not be so.

We wouldn't give a hammer and a chisel to a novice and expect them to produce work worthy of a skilled cabinetmaker. We don't give paint and brushes to a beginner and expect him/her to knock out a masterpiece. So we certainly shouldn't expect children to turn into competent members of a modern complex society without the basic skills of literacy and numeracy.

I well remember going to a parent/teacher meeting with my daughter and having the traditional one-to-one chat with her English teacher. The teacher in question was a bright, enthusiastic young woman who was full of praise for my daughter's indisputable creative powers. Toward the end of the session, I tentatively raised the question of what seemed to me my daughter's tenuous grasp of grammar and punctuation. The teacher laughed, a little condescendingly I thought.

"Those are just examples of non-standard English. We certainly don't wish to stifle your daughter's creativity, now do we?" she said, going on to explain that, up and down the country, the language was evolving and that applying rules and, in particular, finding mistakes, was utterly old school and unacceptable.

I listened for a while to her diatribe – and then I fought back. I told her that language was the most refined tool we had for communicating and that precision in its use was essential for clarity; that while it was true that language evolved, it was also true that, at any given time, there had to be a consensus on what was correct and what wasn't; that sentences which contained unintended ambiguities or, worse still, didn't actually make sense, were an abuse of language; that not knowing when to insert a full stop was like driving a runaway train into the buffers at a crowded station.

My daughter and her teacher smirked, clearly concluding I was some kind of lunatic.

When the smirking ended, I quietly mentioned that I was someone who recruited people like my daughter, when their formal education was concluded, into well-paid, satisfying jobs, and that I expected candidates for such jobs to be able to read and write.

They were both unimpressed but that's par for the course with teenage daughters and, I fear, with teachers unfamiliar with the world of non-academic work.

Anyway, cut me some slack – and read on.

4.3.1 Communicating in writing

Whatever your goal, you are likely, on occasions, to be involved in communicating through the written word. Sadly, skill in this form of communication has been on the wane in recent years.

There are three basic principles that should guide you:

- clarity
- simplicity
- brevity

You must have noticed when reading instructions on products you have bought, or perusing newspaper articles on subjects that interest you, or trying to interpret and complete the interminable flow of forms with which we are all inundated, that the art of writing well – with clarity, simplicity and brevity – went into decline long ago. Ambiguity, jargon, poor punctuation and verbiage abound.

The pharmacist who boldly claims that he dispenses with accuracy only means half of what he's said. The report that "the brave householder ran downstairs and confronted the burglar in his pyjamas" raises more questions than it answers. The sign that reads "Maternity Hospital –

deliveries round the back" raises a smile. And who will ever forget Lynne Truss' homicidal panda who, on departing the murder scene, later explained to the police, "I'm the one that eats, shoots and leaves."

We have to put up with the literary incompetence of others, but we should not add to it ourselves. If we can achieve clarity, simplicity and brevity in our own writing, we seriously increase the chances that the recipient will understand what we have said and, if we are asking or instructing them to do something, that they will do it.

4.3.1.1 Clarity

The more clearly you express yourself, the more likely it is that you will communicate effectively. Always read through what you have written and ask yourself the following questions:

- Is there a way to rearrange each sentence to make my meaning clearer?
- Is there any way the reader could misinterpret or misunderstand what I have written?

4.3.1.2 Simplicity

As a general principle, you should aim to express your meaning as simply as possible. It is almost always counterproductive to use longer words and more complex sentences than is absolutely necessary. Such practices will not impress your reader; rather they will suggest that you are desperately trying to appear more intelligent than you are (assuming that is possible) and that you are using verbiage to cover up a lack of clarity in your thought processes (heaven forbid).

Ask the following questions:

- Could I say exactly the same thing in fewer words?
- Could I use shorter, simpler words to replace longer words without losing meaning?
- Could I simplify my sentence structure and still convey the same meaning?

Of course, some thoughts are more complex than others, so even when such thoughts have been expressed as simply as possible, they may still be difficult to grasp. "As simply as possible" does not always mean simple. Nevertheless, the principle is sound and most ideas, however complex, can generally be broken down into fairly simple, comprehensible elements.

4.3.1.3 Brevity

It follows from the principles of clarity and simplicity that we should aim for brevity – in the sense that the document should be no longer than is necessary to convey the meaning clearly and simply. Using long words or complex sentence structures for their own sake is counterproductive. When it is used in a forlorn attempt to impress, it is generally tedious and often embarrassing. When it is employed to cover up lazy thinking or an inability to think clearly, it damages the author's credibility. Whatever the motivation behind it, verbosity generally impedes understanding, and for that reason alone, brevity is a worthy objective.

There is another reason to aim for brevity, a reason with which anyone who presents to an audience will probably be familiar. We live in a multimedia world where most people have a strictly limited attention span. Unless the audience is interested and entertained, eyes glaze over very quickly.

At home, we are all offered a splendid choice of information, education and entertainment, but if we become bored, even if the presenter has a brain the size of the planet and is expressing an insight for which Einstein would have given his eye teeth, at the press of a button we can and will dismiss him/her from our presence.

So be warned and be brief.

4.3.1.4 Advice on emails

Because of its speed and convenience, the email has to a large extent replaced the letter in business communications, but we should be aware that emails lack the status and impact of the more formal letter, with its letterhead and logo.

This demotion of the formal written missive, combined with the reduced attention span of the average person, means that we should be aware of the email's limitations as a means of communication.

Here are my suggestions.

(1) Give the email a title that indicates the scope of its subject. If it's about more than one subject, consider preparing separate emails for each subject.

(2) In any email, if you are making more than one point, separate and number each point. Otherwise, frequently, you will find the recipient has registered only the first point or, at best, only the first two. Make your points as clearly, simply and briefly as possible.

(3) Copy the email to anyone involved in the subject of the email, even if they are not personally required to do anything. First, this ensures all involved are kept informed. Secondly, it enhances the chances that the recipient will act promptly, knowing that any failure to act will be widely known.

4.3.1.5 Selectivity, a word of warning

Knowing when to put things in writing is a crucial business skill.

A written communication is an excellent means of passing on information, of issuing an instruction, of explaining a situation.

It is also a record. It can protect you – and it can harm you. **Think before you write.** A written record of what you say and to whom you say it can turn out to be your best friend – or your worst enemy.

4.4 NUMERACY

I have often admired the mystical way of
Pythagoras, and the secret magic of numbers.
Religio Medici, Sir Thomas Browne

Don't panic. We're not talking higher maths. But you will need a basic level of numeracy.

First of all, you should see numbers as your friends. Numbers are honest and reliable, not like words, which can be ambiguous and, in the mouth of a liar, misleading and deceitful.

So why do you need to feel at home with elementary maths? Because whether you're doing the weekly shop or negotiating a major contract, you need to know what you are committing yourself to. And that usually involves numbers.

Apart from being able to add, subtract, multiply and divide, it is useful to be adept in calculating percentages. Of course, calculators will do this for you, but it is useful to understand the relationship between the numbers. Here's a little test.

What percentage is 36 of 90? Don't use the percentage key on your calculator.

How did it go? Divide 36 by 90 (= 0.40). This represents the proportion 36 is of 90. Multiply the result by 100: i.e. 0.4 x 100 = 40, to generate the percentage (i.e. 40.0%).

That's the level of maths you need. Here's another one.

By what percentage do you need to increase 36 to reach 90?

Divide 90 by 36 (= 2.50) which tells how many 36s there are in 90. Subtract 1 from the result (2.50 – 1.00 = 1.50) Why? Because that 1 represents the 36 that is given and is the 36 we need to increase to reach 90. In other words, we need another one and a half 36s (i.e. 54) to reach 90. To convert to a percentage, multiply 1.50 by 100 (= 150). So we need to increase 36 by 150% to reach 90 (i.e. 36 + (36 x 1.5 = 54) = 90).

Just to check that it feels right, calculate a 100% increase (i.e. double 36) = 72. To reach 90, we need another 18, which is exactly half of 36, so it looks like the answer of 150% is correct.

Try this one:

What is 70% of 90?

Multiply 70 by 90 = 6,300 and divide the result by 100 to produce the percentage; i.e. 63%. Or even easier: multiply 90 by .7 = 63 (because .7 of anything is 70% of it).

And one last one:

If the invoice total, including VAT, was £90 and the VAT was 20%, what was the cost excluding VAT?

You want to know what number of pounds which, when increased by 20%, would give you £90. Simply divide the £90 by 120 (= 0.75) and multiply by 100 (= 75). So £75 is the cost, excluding VAT. Why divide £90 by 120? Because the £90 is 120% of the figure we are looking for? Why multiply the result by 100? Because 0.75 x 100 gives us the figure (75) which, when you add another 20%, will give us 90. (20% of 75 is 15. 15 + 75 = 90.)

It is not unusual for people to think the answer to the above problem is not £75, but £72. They calculate 80% of £90 (£90 x 0.80) = £72, assuming the £18 difference (£90 − £72 = £18) is the correct figure for VAT, and that £72 is the cost, excluding VAT. They are wrong. If you increase £72 by 20%, you get £86.40 (£72 x 1.2 = £86.40), not £90, whereas increasing £75 by 20% (£75 x 1.2) gives you £90.[1]

Yes, percentages can be confusing, but with practice they become easier to calculate – and it's worth the effort.

Long ago, I recall sitting in a hotel room in Jeddah, in the Kandara Palace Hotel, with my Saudi agent, negotiating a price for a documentary film. My company had set a limit to the amount of commission Saudi agents could demand for their services. For the type of film we were proposing, the limit was 15%. This was the most we reckoned we should pay for the services of the agent and for the support services he was providing.

I had prepared a proposal for the film and priced it, including all production costs to which I had added a small contingency (5%), the company's overhead charges (35%) and a profit (10%). The total came to £87,000. I then added

---

[1] In the above paragraph, I'm using 0.80 instead of 80% and 1.20 instead of 120%. This saves me from having to multiply my results by 100 – and is a useful short cut in calculating percentages.

£13,000 for the agent, giving a price of £100,000, so that his commission would be 13% of the total. (I was hoping to keep the agent's commission a little below the 15% maximum.)

After we had settled down to drink some Arab tea, Mahmoud, the agent, asked how much the film would cost. I told him that it would cost £100,000. "And how much commission?" he enquired.

"Thirteen percent," I replied. "That's £13,000."

"That is not enough," said Mahmoud. Mr Rafi, Mahmoud's Pakistani secretary who accompanied his boss on such occasions, looked nervous.

At this point, there was a power cut. All the lights went out. The sun had set rather abruptly so we were plunged into darkness. We searched a desk and found a couple of candles. This was a time when everyone smoked, so we were able to light the candles immediately.

"I shall need £30,000 on this deal," said Mahmoud flatly. I could see his soft brown eyes in the flickering candlelight. His expression conveyed, through the smoke-filled atmosphere, an unsubtle blend of greed and determination.

"Why?" I asked, just a little irritated.

"I am incurring heavy costs as your agent," said Mahmoud, "and I shall need at least £30,000."

I noticed that £30,000 had already become "at least £30,000." I thought it best to introduce a little sanity into the conversation.

"I can't agree to or authorise a commission of £30,000," I said.

"Yes you can," said Mahmoud. "Just add £17,000 to the price."

"No I can't," I replied, realising we were on the edge of a pantomime exchange of contradictory assertions.

"I can't justify it, and in any case, when my company submits its accounts, our auditors would query that level of remuneration for an agent. Fifteen percent is the top limit."

Mahmoud was finding all this difficult to understand. He clearly thought I had failed to grasp the beautiful simplicity of "just add £17,000 to the price."

"But you are getting what you want," said Mahmoud. "Just add another £17,000 for me."

"Let me explain," I continued wearily. "If I were to pay you £30,000, I couldn't just add £17,000 to the price. If I agreed to pay you £30,000 on a film project valued at £117,000, I would be paying you a commission of a little over 25% – more than 10% above the company's limit of 15%."

Mahmoud was utterly bemused. Ever eager to help, I quickly worked out the price of a film that could legitimately pay Mahmoud £30,000. It wasn't difficult. "We would have to increase the price of the film to £200,000 (i.e. double the price) to pay you £30,000. Only then would £30,000 commission be just within the limit of 15% of the price."

I realised that I was witnessing a true meeting of cultures. Sadly, on this occasion, there was no meeting of minds.

Nevertheless, in such a situation (and indeed in many others), someone has to have a grasp of basic maths.

4.5 EMPATHY

Before you judge others, walk a mile in their shoes.
A version of a Cherokee proverb

Given the emphasis I have put on focusing on core objectives, it may seem odd that in considering core abilities, I put the highest value on empathy – the ability to identify with another person so as to be able to understand their thoughts and feelings.

While empathy is a core skill of the greatest importance it can also be the most difficult for a highly focused and determined individual to exercise.

I have met two or three people in my business career who have an uncanny ability to empathise effortlessly with those they meet. They seem somehow able to lock into the other person's mind and know exactly what they are thinking and feeling. They immediately put the other person at ease. They create the impression that they both understand the other person and are "on their side." The best salespeople have this ability.

We all know the assertive salesman and the tricks they employ. There's the assumption that you have decided to buy:

> "So how would you like to pay – cash or monthly payments?"

> "Which do you prefer – the green or the blue one?"

Or they exert pressure to close a deal:

> "Take your time – but I must tell you this special offer ends this week."

> "It's up to you but this is the last one."

But the really successful salesperson gets inside the prospective purchaser's head and looks at the situation from the purchaser's point of view. They don't exert pressure. They discern what the purchaser wants and then they offer the purchaser the best that their company can do to satisfy that want. The purchaser senses that the salesperson understands them and is eager to help them and is not simply concerned with closing a sale to earn a commission.

The value of empathy in selling is obvious but it is also of inestimable value in every other area of business and, indeed, life. Whether you are arguing with a friend, motivating or disciplining staff, negotiating a deal, or simply presenting a case, the ability to empathise with the other party gives you an insight into how they are thinking and is, therefore, a major advantage in achieving your goal.

What can you do to develop your empathic capacity? It's a good question. I'm not a naturally empathic person. I don't have a gift for easily slipping into somebody else's mind. I have to work at it. So here's what I do. It's not perfect and results can't be guaranteed but it helps and it's a good mental exercise.

When I was at school I was an enthusiastic member of the debating society. On one occasion, just before a general election, the school decided to run a mock election. Mr Craddock, an excellent Classics teacher familiarly known as Chuck, who was chairman of the society, asked me to represent one of the main parties. I agreed. Then he said I was to represent the Conservative Party. At that age, in common with most young thinking kids, I was left of centre.

"Oh!" I said. "I was rather hoping I could represent Labour."

"Why?" he asked, knowing the answer.

"Because if I had a vote, I'd vote Labour."

"That's why I want you to speak for the Conservatives," he replied. "This is a debating society. I want you to come up with the best case you can devise to persuade your friends to vote for the party you don't support."

It was an odd task and one I found difficult, but I set to

work. I studied the party manifestos that had been published in preparation for the real election and put my case together. As I did this, I began to see into the Conservative mind. Conservatives, like Labour, were full of good intentions. True, they had different priorities, different policies and different ways of achieving them, but in terms of objectives, the two parties weren't so very far apart. It opened up for me a new way of thinking. It required me to empathise with the other. It involved a degree of role playing, and although the situation was artificial, the insights were real.

So that's my tip for enhancing your empathic capability. Whether you are motivating or disciplining staff, or negotiating a deal, or simply arguing a case, think of how you would feel if you were the other party. How would you react to what you are saying if you were them, if you were the one to whom it was being said? What arguments would you deploy if you were them? How would you feel about the situation if you were them?

In that mock election of long ago, I realised something else. The way we vote is largely determined by how we see other people. For example:

> View (A) Given healthcare and education, people are, in the main, independent members of society, capable of looking after themselves and their families, and of achieving some degree of social mobility. Given health services, education, and equality of opportunity, people and society thrive best in a meritocratic system, underpinned by a welfare system for those who, through no fault of their own, need state help.

> View (B) Because of the unequal distribution of wealth and the class system, there are inevitably

strict limits within our society to social mobility, meaning that the poor are trapped in poverty. There is therefore an irrefutable need for the redistribution of wealth from the rich to the poor through the tax system, and for widespread and continuous state intervention to ameliorate the worst aspects of deprivation and other forms of social injustice.

Those who take the first view (A) tend to vote right of centre; those who take the second view (B) tend to vote left of centre. These two paragraphs are of course fairly crude statements of the basic attitudes that underpin the philosophies of the two main political parties in the UK. In fact, and in practice, there is a very considerable degree of overlap between the Conservatives and Labour, at least when they are in power. Both parties believe in redistribution of wealth through a progressive tax system. Both believe in equality of opportunity. Both spend much of the country's revenues on a welfare system. Both put health and education at the top of the domestic agenda. That said, there are differences of emphasis and policy – and which party you support depends upon whether your view of people is more in line with paragraph (A) or paragraph (B).

So when we attempt to empathise with other people, we should not only put ourselves in their position, we should also try to understand the attitudes that are likely to determine the other person's responses. If we can do that, we may not agree – indeed we may still find the gap between us unbridgeable – but at least we will understand why they think as they do, why there is a gap and how best to deal with their response.

5
CORE SKILLS

Any fool can know. The point is to understand.
Albert Einstein

I said at the beginning that I was unable to offer any magic tricks, any gimmicks; that I had no silver bullet, no new management technique, no uniquely innovative approach to problem-solving, no catchy sound bite that says it all.

I was being honest but perhaps a little unfair to myself. There are a few techniques that I have acquired, discovered or devised which have helped me to achieve my goals. Some are obvious, some obscure, some are counterintuitive. All have served me well. See what you think.

5.1 PRIORITISING

Of course I set priorities, but I have so many priorities I don't know where to start.
A member of staff at Panarc

5.1.1 The urgent v. the important

Anyone who has set up and run a business or who has managed a department in any organisation will know how easy it is to allow the urgent to take precedence over the important. Indeed it is a major problem to which there is no entirely satisfactory answer. Very often, if something is urgent, then by definition it has to be done quickly. In situations where you have limited resources, you will often have to abandon the important in order to fulfil the requirements of the urgent.

But when the urgent has been resolved, remember to return to the important whenever you can. It is true that often the important is difficult. It requires real mental effort and, quite possibly, substantial resources. But it is worth doing because, by definition, dealing with the important is likely to bring far greater benefits than meeting any particular deadline.

In running my media coverage analysis business there were often occasions when we had an important project in hand to refine the computer program that analysed the coverage. The improvement might have centred on a more sensitive way of measuring the effect of coverage on its target audience, or a better way of quantifying the reach of the coverage, or some other valuable enhancement. But there was always competition for time and resources from the urgent. There was always coverage to be coded, existing data to be analysed, and reports to be written and delivered to a deadline.

Of course, we had to meet deadlines (we never missed one in thirty-two years). So the really important project would have to be temporarily postponed – postponed, but not abandoned. Analysing media coverage is not easy;

reliably assessing the impact of coverage on the audience it reaches is difficult. Refining and enhancing the Max program was a never-ending task. We were convinced the quality of the service we offered depended on the integrity of our analytical techniques and the quality of our software. Most important of all, it was the key to our belief in the service we offered.

5.1.2 Lists

I'm a strong believer in lists; in particular, in lists of things to do.

A simple note pad with a list of tasks in some kind of order (e.g. in order of importance, or in time order) will do for a start. Such lists help to focus the mind on what needs to be done, discourage time-wasting on irrelevancies and give the user a feeling of satisfaction when tasks are completed. A typical To-Do list form will look like this:

Priority	Task	Tick

If you spend five minutes every morning preparing a list of the tasks you hope to complete that day, and then during the day, work your way through the list, you will be surprised how much more you can get done. Put the list in order of priority so that if you run out of time, you will at least have completed the most important tasks.

For those who wish to take the To-Do list idea further, there is software available which will help you to organise and manage your own and others' work schedules. (Take a look at To-Do list software and the various task management systems.)

That said, a simple sheet of paper with a table showing tasks and priorities will quickly, simply, and cheaply prove the usefulness of working this way.

5.1.3 Whose priority?

Here's a thought! Your priorities are not necessarily the same as those of other people. This is obviously true, but when working under pressure, it's easily forgotten.

When Panarc became involved in the publishing business, we were often asked to organise the mass distribution of books. For one project, we were tasked with sending thousands of books to libraries, academic and governmental institutions, and eminent politicians around the world. Each package had to contain:

- a copy of the book in the appropriate language
- a covering letter explaining the purpose of the book and why we were sending it to the recipient
- an envelope containing the letter, personally addressed to the recipient

And the despatch of the books had to be timed to coincide with promotion of the book.

We didn't have the staff or the space to perform all these tasks in-house, so we looked for a distribution company that could handle the job.

But there was a problem. We had to make sure all the tasks were done correctly and on time. Obviously we had to be sure that the correct letter was inserted in the right envelope if we were sending a copy of the book to a head of state or a minister.

The distribution company assured us that all would be well, but on further questioning, we established that this was not a run-of-the-mill assignment for them. Their distribution system was automated but not set up to insert letters in envelopes, much less to check that the right letters went into the right envelopes. What's more, they had many other regular clients who would not take kindly to any interruption to their distribution requirements that our more complicated project might cause.

We discussed the problem with the distribution company and it seemed we might have to look elsewhere. Their priorities were not ours.

We found a solution. I and two of my staff went to the company's premises, got to know the staff, and persuaded the manager to allow us to help with the distribution. He had the benefit of extra staff, free of charge, and we were able to make sure the work was done to our standard.

So, when your priorities are not the same as those of someone you are relying on to perform a task for which you are ultimately responsible, don't trust to luck. Either find someone who can give your task the level of priority you need, or find another way to ensure your requirements are met.

In 1975, when I started marketing sponsored documentary films for Visnews in Saudi Arabia, it was like being in the middle of a gold rush. I had been sent by the Visnews MD to find out what Maurice Thompson, Visnews Middle East sales executive, was getting up to. He had been in the Kingdom for several weeks but, to date, there had been no sales and the only paperwork was his rather alarming expense claims arriving by telex in Visnews Head Office.

When I landed at Riyadh Airport, I was greeted by Maurice and a sweet, noxious aroma ensuing from the open sewer that ran down the middle of Riyadh's main street. There was only one hotel for foreign visitors, the Al Yamamah. On the taxi drive from the airport to the hotel, I could see we were driving through an enormous, hot, sunbaked building site. When we reached the hotel, it was packed with businessmen from all over the world engaged in intense conversations with Saudi agents. The snippets of conversation I picked up seemed to consist entirely of very large numbers and percentages.

"We have a reservation," I said when I reached the front desk.

"We are full," said the harassed receptionist, a smartly dressed Pakistani.

"But we have a reservation," I repeated, slightly alarmed.

"You have a reservation. Everyone has a reservation," said the receptionist. "You can sleep in the foyer."

Maurice intervened, and eventually we were allocated a large but dirty room in a generally unused corner of the hotel. I began to understand why Maurice's expenses seemed excessive.

My understanding was further enhanced when I succeeded in closing our first film contract. As our Saudi agent was involved, I needed to confirm with Visnews the terms I had agreed with the agent. We went to a small back office that housed the hotel's only telex machine. I handed the text for my telex, neatly written on the hotel's telex form, to the telex operator and asked him to send it urgently. He shrugged, indicating a foot-high pile of similar telex forms. He inserted my telex at the bottom.

"When will you send my telex?" I asked.

The telex operator shrugged. "Two or three days maybe."

"But I need it sent today," I insisted. I had a meeting with the Deputy Minster the following day to finalise the contract.

There was a pause. It was my first visit to the Kingdom and it took me a moment to realise what was expected of me. We had entirely different priorities. Mine was to finalise Visnews' first contract in the Kingdom; his was to exploit for his own benefit the financial opportunity presented by the laws of supply and demand. I took out my wallet and offered him what I thought could be construed as either a generous tip or a modest bribe. The telex operator retrieved my telex form and moved it from the bottom of the pile to a position about a third of the way up. For just over double what I had first offered, my telex rose to the top of the pile. I decided to wait until he had sent it, just in case some other businessmen arrived with urgent telexes, deeper wallets and higher priorities than mine.

5.2 QUALITY v. SPEED

> *Had we but world enough and time*
> "To his Coy Mistress," Andrew Marvell

I'm assuming that, at this stage, you are focused, determined and hardworking. In other words, you have the key qualities that will bring you success. But I have to ask you an important question.

Are you a one-speed person (i.e. can you work only at a fixed pace)?

There is nothing inherently wrong in being a one-speed person. In many areas of life it is no disadvantage. If you work on a production line, you are likely to cause trouble if you work faster than the pace agreed with the union. If you are an artist and, to meet your exacting standards, you can only work at one speed, it doesn't matter (although it may mean you produce fewer masterpieces). And there are some administrative tasks where avoiding errors is paramount, and it would be unwise to ask anyone to speed up because it would imperil accuracy.

But in business it does matter. Successful business people have learned to strike the optimum balance between quality and speed. And they need to learn how to do this because that is what they have to do every day of their lives.

If you're not a variable-speed person, work on it. Pick any task that you routinely perform and see how long it takes. Then see if you can reduce that time when you next perform the task. If you try harder, you will be surprised what you can achieve. You may also discover ways of performing the task not merely more quickly, but also more efficiently – a double bonus. Get into the habit of trying this experiment with different types of task. It's a good discipline and will improve your general performance.

Good is good; but good and quick is better.

5.2.1 Deadlines

> *But at my back I always hear*
> *Time's wingéd chariot hurrying near.*
> "To His Coy Mistress," Andrew Marvell

Everything has a deadline, including life itself. We all have an allotted span. We all have hopes and ambitions. So we all know that there is a limit to the time we have to sustain our hopes and to fulfil our ambitions.

In business, there are deadlines everywhere for everything. Projects have to be completed, reports delivered, goods despatched by a certain time. Often we have to work under pressure. Often the time we have to complete, deliver or despatch is less than, in ideal circumstances, we would need.

So we can either miss the deadline, work faster or edit the work to fit the time available.

We don't want to miss the deadline, although in some professions and some circumstances, we may have to. (Some projects involve processes that cannot be accelerated and safety procedures that cannot be truncated. For such, we have to insist on an extension of the deadline.)

Excluding such cases, if we can work faster, the problem is solved.

It's the third solution that merits further comment because it requires an ability which is invaluable but which, for some, is impossible.

How can you edit the work to fit the time available? What is this editing?

Let's say first of all what it isn't. It certainly isn't doing the job at normal pace and just not finishing it. A project delivered that is only 80% complete has not met the deadline.

Nor does it mean cutting corners, i.e. doing everything the project requires but badly.

What it means is standing back from the project and reassessing it. It requires the mental exercises described in 4.2 The Organising Mind. List the tasks involved, hierarchise them, identify those that are most important and allocate them the necessary time. For the rest, either perform them as best you can in the remaining time or omit them, noting that they have been omitted for lack of time. The key question is this: at the end, is it fair to say you have completed the project by the deadline? Of course, it may not be done as well as it would have been had you had more time, but is it the best achievable given the time available?

In short, we're back to précis-ing the task (see 2.4 Bettering):

> **You need to précis tasks, just as you précis articles.** If there isn't time to perform the whole task to 99% perfection, then précis the task and perform **the key elements of the whole task** to the **highest level you can in the time available.**

For some, this is a natural way of dealing with the inevitable time pressures that we are all subjected to in business. Others learn how to do it. But there are some for whom, sadly, it is not natural or learnable. They can still be successful, but they will have to achieve success despite this gap in their skill set.

5.2.2 The perfect v. the good

Have no fear of perfection – you'll never reach it.
Salvador Dali

There is a popular saying that pithily summarises this section.

"Let not the perfect be the enemy of the good."

Don't fail to deliver good work simply because you aspire to achieve perfection.

There are some spheres of life where this maxim does not apply (e.g. purely creative endeavour), and in every sphere of life we should aim to do the best we can (i.e. where good is simply not good enough). But there is some truth in this adage. Perfection is out of reach, so the quest for it should never be an excuse for failure to deliver.

In business, there is always pressure and we have to find a sensible compromise between the pursuit of excellence and getting the job done. It's simple. As noted elsewhere, you should always do the very best you can with the resources you have in the time available.

5.3 LISTENING

We have two ears and one mouth as a gentle hint that we should spend twice as much time listening as we do talking.

(Thank you, Epictetus)

Listening deserves its own section. I have nothing particularly original to say about listening, in either life or business, but it is surprisingly important and most people find it exceedingly difficult to follow the rules. Almost everyone likes to talk; sadly, they are less inclined to listen.

We all feel that what we have to say is profoundly interesting, and almost certainly far more riveting and probably more important than what that other fellow is saying. "He's certainly gone on far too long. Most of what he says is off the point. He's irritatingly verbose, imprecise, and incoherent." That's what we think. And often we are right.

In many social situations, when people talk, they have an agenda. They are eager to tell you something about themselves.

The intended message may be that they are clever, kind, rich, enlightened, witty, or any one of an almost limitless list of positive attributes that will bolster their image. Some feel the need to compete with others in almost any circumstance. If you've bought a new car, they cannot wait to tell you that their new car is bigger or better. If you've been on a delightful cruise round the Mediterranean, they feel compelled to tell you all about their world cruise, which was so good the first time that they've just repeated it.

In business, things are much the same, except that this human inclination toward self-obsession and self-promotion actually adversely affects the running of the business. The tendency to self-promote, to compete with other individuals or departments, often runs counter to the need for interdepartmental cooperation and focus on key goals. At best, it's a dreadful waste of time; at worst, it can divert energy, money, and other resources away from the business's core objective.

So the first piece of advice is simple – don't be a self-obsessed, self-promoting "boil on the heel of progress."[2]

Secondly, listen actively, not passively. Don't think of listening as the idle, rather boring periods between the fascinating nuggets of information that you are eager to contribute to the conversation. And don't imagine you are listening just because you aren't talking. Instead, listen attentively; register what others are saying; analyse it; critique it; exploit it. **You can learn a great deal from what people say, a great deal more than what is said.** Ask yourself why they are saying what they are saying. Are they trying to

---

[2] This is a quote from a long-forgotten second-rate cowboy film starring Dan Duryea, who delivers this delightful metaphor before shooting dead his injured criminal buddy.

impress you, persuade you, probe you? What are the drivers that motivate them?

The practice of listening actively is particularly valuable in business. There is a lot of misdirection in business, some intentional, some subconscious. Many employees pay lip service to the official corporate goals while ruthlessly and persistently pursuing their own agenda. Listening often gives you clues to what really motivates the other person.

Don't think that you always need to talk. As Plato remarked: "Wise men talk because they have something to say; fools, because they have to say something." It's a good principle to say nothing if you have nothing to say. **Shallow waters tend to babble; still waters run deep.**

And remember, other people love listeners. I discovered this in my youth when meeting girls. If I gave them the opportunity to tell me about themselves, they would often chat happily for hours, encouraged only by the occasional nod or grunt. Then, frequently (and when it first happened, inexplicably) I would get feedback from a mutual friend that the girl found me really interesting, even though I had said next to nothing.

So learn to listen. And listen to learn.

5.4 INDIRECTION

In-off: a shot that goes into a pocket after striking another ball

Collins Dictionary definition of a
term used in billiards

Indirection is the term I use for conveying a message to someone through a third party (i.e. indirectly). It is a useful technique in both social and business life.

The problem with direct, one-to-one communication is that people aren't always honest (harsh but true). Of course, there's a whole spectrum of deceit, from a mild distortion of the facts through to a barefaced lie, but we always have to be aware in social and commercial intercourse that those with whom we're chatting may not be speaking the truth, much less the whole truth and nothing but the truth. And, indeed, they in turn may suspect that we are not being totally honest either. For example, we may say to a superior that we greatly admire her management style. She may doubt our sincerity (especially just before a salary review), thinking we are simply flattering her for some ulterior motive.

Funnily enough, one way to firm up someone's confidence in the truth of what we say is to say it also to others, others whom our doubting, suspicious superior knows well. With a little luck, these others will report to their friend that you have told him that you greatly admire her management style. The fact that you are expressing your admiration to others will help to convince her of your sincerity.

Indeed, quite often, you can omit the direct communication altogether. Don't tell your superior you admire her management style. Just tell her friend.

In my youth, I discovered this was by far the best way of making out with girls. Rather than telling the girl how much I liked her (which could have attracted the "ulterior motive" suspicion), it was often better to tell one of her friends. To share such a confidence with someone else gave the sentiment a (deserved, of course) aura of authenticity.

Used sparingly and carefully, indirection can be a powerful weapon in the communications armoury.

(Author's note: In advocating listening and indirection, it will be clear that some of the more sophisticated techniques I recommend were discovered in my youth and derived not from business but from a genuine interest in and preoccupation with girls. This should not in any way diminish their relevance to achieving success in the commercial world.)

5.5 TIMING

For perfect timing, simply choose the moment between too soon and too late.

Anon.

A major factor in achieving success is timing. Making the right decision can be hard, but getting the timing right is often harder.

The stock market provides an excellent example. Even a novice investor can follow the trends and see when there is a bull or a bear market. The market is cyclical, so the investor can be reasonably sure that a bull market will turn into a bear market at some point. But when? If she cashes in her stocks too early, she will miss out on growth of the bull market. If he leaves it too late, he will be caught in a bear market and the value of his investments will tumble. Investors know what will happen. But the question is: when?

Timing is crucial in many of life's decisions: when to ask for a rise … when to change jobs … when to propose marriage … when to have children … when to raise a difficult or sensitive issue … when to talk … when to be silent, etc. In all these cases, getting the timing right can be the difference between success and failure.

And it's not just the timing of decisions that is important. The pace at which you deliver a presentation can make the difference between captivating an audience and boring them to death. Timing in the delivery of a punchline to a joke (and in comedy in general) can make all the difference between a hearty laugh and an undisguised yawn.

So, if it's so important, how can we improve our timing? The answer is simple. Take into account all the many factors that have a bearing on the issue, weight them according to their importance, take into account any synergistic effects, factor in the mental state of everyone else involved, bear in mind everything else that is going on and assess its likely effect on how your actions will be received. Then arrange all these factors on a timeline and simply choose the optimal moment to make the decision.

And that's why **timing, like the weather, is difficult to get right.**

My only advice is this. At least think about it. In personal relationships, most of us have a feel for when the time is right, a faculty often developed painfully by trial and error. In business, at least try to identify and assess the main factors that have a bearing on the case. Often, when we have decided "something has to be said or done", we act too quickly. So pause. Equally, when we have been unable to decide whether something has to be said or done, we can be too slow. So think about it, and then get on with it.

When investing in the stock market, take a long-term view.

5.6 MOTIVATING

Success consists of going from failure to failure without loss of enthusiasm.

Winston Churchill

There's always the stick and the carrot.

In recent times, the stick has fallen out of favour. According to current wisdom, carrots are the thing. Don't just pay people for the work they do; show that you appreciate them and care for them. Encourage a positive *esprit de coeur* among your staff. Be open and honest with them. Involve them in discussions about issues affecting the business. Listen to them and show respect for the contribution they make. Employees are people with their own lives, not just automata that must do your bidding. Accept that they all, men and women, need to establish a satisfactory work/life balance. If you do this, they will be happier, more highly motivated, more likely to remain healthy, less likely to become depressed or quit. They will be more productive. It's a win–win situation.

There is, of course, a great deal of truth in the above – and it is certainly a better approach than the stick-wielding tyrant of yesteryear. My only very minor quibble with this approach is that it tends to discourage discrimination between those who are really good – i.e. those who are particularly talented and work particularly hard – and those who aren't and don't.

I know. I know – everyone is talented in some way; everyone works hard. But if you've ever run a business, you know that in reality some people are twice as productive as others. Some take responsibility willingly; others do all they can to avoid it. Some go the extra mile; others have their coats on before the bell goes. Some people see solutions to problems; others see only the problem.

So there's no harm, and no doubt some good, in repeating the mantra, "Everyone is talented in some way. Everyone works hard," but we should never forget that it just isn't true.

If you've come with me this far, you are almost certainly someone who is at least twice as productive as the average person. You are goal-orientated, focused, determined and hardworking. You are, therefore, probably in a minority of about 10% of the working population. You are the perfect employee. And, with the ability to reason, to listen, and to show empathy, you are probably an excellent employer.

Remember this: only the few succeed; you are one of the few.

5.7 PERCEPTION AND REALITY

If perception was reality, the straight stick in
water that looks bent would really be bent.

Anon.

Now I think it only fair to say at this point that you may not like, much less agree with, the content of this section. Following on from the previous section (5.6: Motivating), it identifies what I think is a bit of a problem, for all its other manifest virtues, with modern thinking. But read on, because it's a problem that I think you can exploit to your advantage.

When running my media coverage analysis business, on occasions someone would produce a piece of substandard work. The report was badly written; the statistical evidence didn't support the conclusions. Perhaps they had written it on an off-day. Perhaps they were losing interest in the work. Perhaps they really didn't have the ability to meet the necessary standard. I would call the analyst in, go through the report, point out its defects and suggest ways to eliminate them, and explain that if we sent out work of such a standard, we would risk losing clients. I was never aggressive or domineering, but I was honest and frank.

After one or two such instances, my general manager (an extremely able woman who was my deputy) came to see me about my management style. It seemed I had really upset the analyst. I said I was sorry if that was so, but I had to point out the problems.

"Yes," said my deputy, "but you should also praise them as well as criticise them, so that when they leave your office they don't feel so down."

I took what my deputy said on board. And I realised the world had changed. Back in the day (my day, I suppose), you were praised for good work and criticised for bad work. When you were criticised, you didn't go into depression; you resolved to do better. There were standards; you had to meet them. If you fell below the standard, you had to try harder. That was the way it had been at grammar school. That was how I thought I could run my business.

But no. Now everyone was good. Yes, some were better, but all were good. (It made me think, sadly, of *Animal Farm* where all the animals were equal but some were more equal than others.)

This idea that everything is good, that criticism is damaging, is a relatively new phenomenon. It is pervasive.

For twelve years, we provided a media analysis service to one of the UK's biggest companies. Our client was the company's Market Research Group. We used to attend a monthly meeting at which we presented our analysis of their media coverage and they reviewed the results of their monthly Customer Satisfaction Survey.

I had been trained in market research and therefore took a professional interest in their Customer Satisfaction

Survey. They used a ten-point scale to assess customers' experience of the company's service each month. You may be familiar with these types of questions from online surveys:

Indicate your level of satisfaction with the service, where 10 represents Excellent:

	1	2	3	4	5	6	7	8	9	10
Please tick one box										

At the time, the company was going through a rough patch in terms of customer satisfaction. We knew this from our analysis of their media coverage (editorial news coverage, including letters to the editor) which revealed that in many cases there was real anger among customers. So, innocently, I asked whether it wouldn't make more sense to have a bi-polar scale, running from -5 (appalling service) through 0 (neither good nor bad) to +5 (excellent).

	-5	-4	-3	-2	-1	0	+1	+2	+3	+4	+5
Please tick one box											

I guess today many would think I was mad to make such a suggestion, but because of my training, I genuinely thought that the function of market research was to speak truth to power.

But no!

I was taken to one side by one of the senior managers. He conceded that, given public sentiment at the time, a bi-polar scale would certainly have allowed respondents to express their opinion more clearly, but my suggestion had to be rejected because "the board doesn't like bad news."

In other words the truth, like reason, has been demoted in our modern world. I couldn't tell my subordinate that their work was substandard; this company's market research department couldn't tell their superiors that the company's customers were dissatisfied.

Where this tendency to pretend that things are other than they are has come from I'm not entirely sure. Perhaps it is something to do with today's teaching methods. What I do know is this: many young people find the ideas of objective truth and personal accountability both unfamiliar and rather frightening.

"Aha!" you say. "What is objective truth? Perception is reality."

"Aha!" I reply. "No, it isn't – at least not in the way you mean it."

When somebody produces a substandard report (because it is badly written, because the statistical evidence doesn't support the conclusions, because it is poorly structured and incoherent), that is the truth. If we send that report to the client, he is likely to say, "The statistical evidence didn't support the conclusions; it was poorly structured; it is incoherent," and we lose the contract.

If a company's market research people are afraid to tell the board that the service the company provides is so bad that many customers are tearing their hair out, it doesn't change the feelings of the customers. It simply allows the board to live in a bubble of extremely dangerous complacency. If they can, customers will abandon the company in droves.

Perception is deceptive. Reality rules, OK.

And therein lies the advantage for you. There is a real world. There is good and bad; there is winning and losing; there is success and failure. In the end, reality asserts itself.

If those around you choose to live in a world based on self-deception, they are in for a rude awakening. You know the truth – and the truth will make you strong.

If you are building a team, try to find at least some others like yourself who understand that there is a real world out there. In terms of their usefulness in business, they're worth at least twice the average person and I hope you are able to pay them at least twice as much.

5.8 THE TUNNEL AND THE CAVE

> *In the face of an obstacle which it is impossible to overcome, stubbornness is stupid.*
> *The Ethics of Ambiguity*, Simone de Beauvoir

Someone once said: "If there's no light at the end of the tunnel, you're not in a tunnel. You're in a cave." I was amused. It was a witty remark. And then I thought about it again and realised it contained a profound truth.

Throughout this book I have lauded determination. It is often the difference between success and failure. But there has to be a qualification.

Sometimes you will strive with all your determination to achieve a goal but you do not succeed. You do not succeed because you cannot succeed. The goal you have set is impossible. However hard you try, you will fail. You are 5ft 8ins tall, 10 stone, and have poor hand–eye coordination. You are never going to be world heavyweight boxing champion. You aim to become your country's Pavarotti, but you are tone deaf. You aspire to challenge the mathematics behind Einstein's Theory of Relativity, but the last time you did any maths was when, despite extra tuition, you failed your GCSE maths exam.

You have mistaken a cave for a tunnel.

I hasten to add that recognising you are in a cave is not the same as giving up simply because to carry on trying is too hard. No. Cave-recognition is all about accepting reality. You can't spend your life attempting to achieve the impossible. Far better to turn round and make your way out of the cave into the fresh air where you can redefine your goal and devote all your time, energy, and determination to achieving it.

I accept it's not always easy, but when faced with a challenge or a problem about which you can do nothing, move on. If you don't, you will be doubly harmed, once by condemning yourself to failure, and again by denying yourself the opportunity to succeed at something else.

6

NEGOTIATING

*The art of negotiating is reluctantly conceding to the
other party that they should do what you want.*

Anon.

Negotiating is an important part of life. In some form, we
negotiate every day of our lives – with family, with friends,
with strangers, even with ourselves. Again, some people
have a natural talent for it; others struggle. But even those
who struggle can learn the basics and, indeed, some of the
more sophisticated techniques.

Negotiating is an important skill to master (or at least
to gain competence in), not just because it's a skill required
every day but because it powerfully affects our chances of
success. Most life goals require us to engage with other
people, and when we interact with other people, there is
invariably some element of negotiation involved.

6.1 SETTING OBJECTIVES

Let's be clear from the start. Negotiating is not always about winning; indeed, it's rarely about winning in any redneck, unilateral sort of way.

In personal relationships, especially intimate ones, the objective has to be to achieve a high degree of balance. If one person wins and his/her partner loses, there is a problem, not a victory. Persistent imbalance in personal relationships is generally unhealthy and can be seriously damaging. As they say, there has to be give and take, and the aim of the giving and taking is to establish an equilibrium.

In business and politics, the objective is rather different. We are not so much looking for equilibrium as for the best possible outcome for ourselves, **given the relative strengths and weaknesses of our position and that of whomever we are negotiating with**.

First, we need to define our objectives (our core objective and any ancillary objectives) and those of the other party. Exactly what is it, in specific terms, that we want? Exactly what is it the other party wants? At this stage, we should aim high for ourselves. We want everything. We probably won't get it, but it's a good starting point – and it makes any necessary concessions later on less painful. (Indeed, before any negotiating takes place, we should have a clear idea of what concessions we might be persuaded to make and which of our objectives are inviolable.)

We should also attempt to determine why the other party wants what they want. Their motives may affect the way they negotiate and which concessions they can and can't make.

When we're clear about each party's objectives, we can begin to assess the scope of the negotiation, the starting position of each party and the relative importance of the drivers behind the objectives of each party.

Having completed this preparatory work, it is crucially important that, as far as possible, we ensure the attainment of our objectives is central in the negotiating process.

As what will surely become a classic case study, let's take the UK's Brexit negotiations from 2016 to 2019 as our example. I choose it because, at the time of writing, it is dominating the news and because the UK negotiators provide a perfect example of how not to negotiate – and thus an excellent opportunity to illustrate what not to do.

The scope of the negotiation was the departure of the UK from the European Union, following a referendum in the UK in 2016 when, in a high turn-out (72.2% of those eligible to vote), 17.4 million (or 52%) voted to leave the EU while 16.1 million (48%) voted to remain.

The UK establishment was shocked and stunned. In the campaign before the referendum, the entire UK state apparatus had been used to argue that leaving the EU would be an act of serious, if not fatal, national self-harm.

When the result of the referendum was announced, the EU Commission was equally perturbed, as were the leaders of the member states of the EU. If we exclude Greenland (a part of Denmark), no member of the EU had ever left the Union. To the EU, the UK's decision to leave seemed perverse. They were deeply disappointed at the damage the UK would cause. The EU would lose the UK's substantial annual net contributions to the EU's financial resources, and the prestige of having as a member of the EU the world's fifth or sixth largest economy, a permanent member of the UN Security Council, a nuclear power, and the EU's only member to form part of the Five Eyes. The EU was not happy.

UK Objective: Despite much sympathy for the EU's views in the UK Parliament, the UK Government declared that it accepted the result of the referendum and set **leaving the EU in order to regain control of the country's money, borders and laws** as its objective. This meant extricating the UK from the political and judicial institutions of the EU, while seeking a free-trade agreement with the EU.

EU Objective: It was clear from the start that the EU's objective was to ensure that it would be evident to all that any state which decided to leave the EU would have a difficult time. There is strong anti-EU sentiment in the populations of several member countries, and the EU Commission was determined to demonstrate that any country which tried to leave would pay a high price. Ideally, those attempting to leave or objecting to EU treaty changes should be persuaded to think again. When Eire, France and the Netherlands rejected the European Constitution, either the people's view was ignored or the people were asked to vote again until, in the form of the Lisbon Treaty, the European Constitution was approved.

With all this in mind, we now need to turn our attention to the analysis of strengths and weaknesses.

6.2 STRENGTHS AND WEAKNESSES

In any business negotiation, it is essential to draw up a clearly defined list of strengths and weaknesses before initiating the negotiating process. Such a list must focus tightly on the strengths and weaknesses in relation to the negotiation. Each side may have outstanding strengths and weaknesses in a general sense, but we are interested only in those that are directly related to the negotiation issue.

The point of drawing up such a list is to help each side to use its strengths to best advantage and to minimise any weaknesses. Each side needs to assess how strong it will be in the negotiating process, and when, and on what negotiating issue, it should apply its greatest strength. **Each side must aim to use its strengths judiciously, reserving them for the attainment of core objectives**.

Continuing with our example, we will draw up a strengths and weaknesses analysis for the negotiations on the UK's withdrawal from the EU. The list is not exhaustive but it is adequate

- to show how important it is for negotiators to get their minds round the scope of any negotiations
- to identify the major factors likely to determine the outcome
- to indicate the arguments that are likely to carry most weight

UK's Strengths
Major contributor to EU budget (approx. £9–£10 bn a year net)
World's 5th largest economy by GDP
Major importer of EU goods
Global exporter
World leader in provision of financial services
Member of the Five Eyes
Major contributor to global security
Permanent member of the UN Security Council
A nuclear power
First-class diplomatic network

UK's Weaknesses
Disconnect between the UK's political establishment and the people
Victory of Leave over Remain (52% against 48%) definite, but not overwhelming
UK political establishment in favour of remaining in the EU

EU's Strengths
Control of access to the market of the world's largest trading bloc
Trade agreements with fifty countries
Numerous agreements on transnational issues (e.g. climate change, medicines)

EU's Weaknesses
Sluggish growth compared to other major trading blocs
Disconnect in some member states between the Commission (an unelected bureaucracy) and the people

6.3 UNDERSTANDING THE DYNAMICS

There is one other consideration of paramount importance. It is essential to recognise the general nature of the negotiation. Is it a negotiation where the core objective of the parties are aligned, or is it a negotiation where the core objectives are in conflict?

In the former case, it is reasonable to assume goodwill on both sides and both parties can adopt a more conciliatory, compromising approach to negotiations. Good examples of such negotiations are joining a club, buying a car or getting married. In such cases, both parties essentially want the same thing; it is the terms on which the mutually desired objective can be achieved that have to be negotiated.

In the latter case (a conflict negotiation), the parties have to realise that they are in a zero sum game. Any advantage one side gains is at the expense of the interests of the other side. Good examples of this type of negotiation are leaving employment in a company to set up a rival organisation, two countries laying claim to the same land, or two people getting divorced. In such cases, the advantage to one tends to be to the disadvantage of the other.

While running my media analysis business, I became involved in a publishing project. A foreign friend of mine asked me to act on his behalf in dealing with a small but reputable publisher who had undertaken to publish his book. The book was academic but of sufficient general interest to have potential for sales to universities, libraries, and public bodies. My friend, the author, was highly regarded by many of those who would be in a position either to promote or to order the book. He was therefore an essential element in the marketing of the book and crucial to its success.

Simply as a favour to my friend, I agreed to act on his behalf with the publisher. I made contact with Peter, the MD of the publishing house. We got on well. He was a very affable fellow but, as it turned out, blighted by an inability to understand the dynamics of a deal.

The book was published and well received. Sales began to pour in. It was the only serious academic work on its subject and it soon became clear that sales were going to exceed expectations.

I first became aware of a problem when my friend asked me if I could remind Peter to pay him his royalties. I raised the matter with Peter who assured me he would deal with it at once. Some weeks later, my friend contacted me again. No royalties. I went to see Peter. He was perfectly pleasant to me, but he said that he was the publisher and he had no intention of being told what to do by one of his authors. I was very fair. I explained to Peter the role my friend was playing in the marketing of the book and that he was largely responsible for the booming sales. Peter was unmoved.

This is, I think, an extreme case, but it illustrates my point that some people find it difficult to grasp the dynamics of a deal. Peter's ego, his inflated idea of his status as a publisher, led directly to a breakdown of a potentially lucrative relationship between him and my friend.

When I next met my friend, we discussed the situation and agreed the easiest solution would be for us to become partners. I would become his publisher for all future projects. I had some limited experience of publishing (having self-published a couple of my own books), but my greatest merit was that I understood the dynamics of the deal. Royalties were always paid promptly under my management.

This little case study illustrates two points. First, in a negotiation, always be aware that the other party (in this case my friend) can walk away. (If they can't walk away, for them it's not a negotiation – it's a humiliation). Secondly, make sure you understand the nature of the negotiation. The relationship between Peter and my friend turned from a perfectly aligned negotiation into a conflict negotiation, and thus into a zero sum game.

Returning to my running case study of the UK/EU withdrawal negotiations, we find another example of a zero sum game. The UK wanted to leave; the EU wanted the UK to stay. The better the deal the UK negotiated, the worse it was for the interests of the EU. It was, essentially, a conflict negotiation. There were elements of the negotiation where there should have been a common interest. (It was to the benefit of both parties that trade should continue with the minimum of friction.) But the central issue, from the Commission's viewpoint, was that the UK had to be unequivocally worse off outside the EU than in – perhaps even so much worse off that the result of the referendum could be reversed.

There was also an emotional element that should not be ignored. From the EU's point of view, the UK had committed the worst of all sins. It had decided to leave. Given the aspiration of the EU to forge ever closer union between the member states, the UK's decision to leave was the equivalent of despair in Christian theology – i.e. the one unforgivable sin. The EU can accommodate misbehaviour by member states; it can live with unpaid fines for transgression of its rules; it can embrace economies that entirely fail to meet its criteria for membership. But what it finds utterly unforgivable is the decision of a member state to say: "Yes, we understand what you are, your ambitions and goals, and how you behave and we don't like it. Indeed we dislike it so much we are going to leave." Of course, the EU controlled its anger. With laudable restraint, it expressed regret for the UK's decision. But within the EU Commission, there was the outrage of a woman scorned.

In short, the UK's first mistake was to misunderstand the essential nature of the negotiation.

6.3.1 Participants

Having understood (or, in the case of the UK negotiators, misunderstood) the general nature of the negotiations, it is necessary to identify the key players in the negotiation. In many cases, this is easy. There are just two parties. In the case of the Brexit negotiations, the situation was far more complex. There were of course the two obvious participants:

- the UK Government
- the EU Commission, charged by the Council of Ministers to undertake the negotiations

But in this case, there were two other participants:

- the member states of the EU
- the Remainers, the opposition to Brexit in the UK, i.e. almost all the political establishment (including a majority in Parliament) and, of course, almost half the UK population

As it turned out, the Remainers played a peculiar and pivotal role in the negotiations, a role examined in more detail in Section 6.3.3 Power Distribution.

Here we should simply note that the reluctance, if not the refusal, of many Remainers to accept the outcome of the referendum caused the UK government to make yet another negotiating error. The people of the UK had been offered an "in/out" referendum. It was a clear binary choice, leading to a clear unilateral decision. But the UK government was conscious that 48% of the electorate had voted to remain in the EU and that the UK establishment was wholly opposed to leaving. Theresa May, the British Prime Minister, heroically took on the task of negotiating our exit but, perhaps understandably, she made the mistake of trying to appease those who were opposed to Brexit, desperately looking for a middle way. She didn't seem to grasp that a binary choice had been made. She couldn't negotiate a deal that would please both Brexiteers and Remainers any more than a girl can be a little bit pregnant. In the end, her Chequers proposal and the Withdrawal

Agreement pleased almost nobody. Her motion to approve the deal suffered the worst defeat in parliamentary history.

6.3.2 Defining the scope and controlling the language

In the democracy of ancient Greece, a man's ability to influence others with his words was considered a matter of great importance. A politician's expertise in the civic art of rhetoric was viewed as a crucial and much-admired accomplishment.

Today, it is just as important, although the key rhetorical techniques have changed. In the ancient world, the main rhetorical virtues were the ability to reason and to present a case eloquently. Today, it is the ability to encapsulate complex thoughts into simple words or phrases in order to persuade the listener to see things as the speaker wishes them to be seen.

"Redundancies" become "downsizing," "outsourcing," "consolidating" or "rationalising."

Endless programme repeats on television become "another opportunity to see."

"We are going to do something you don't like in future, but not yet" becomes "We have no plans to do this thing you don't like."

"With respect" means "I'm about to prove you're an idiot."

"I hear what you say" means "When you've finished (which I hope is now), I'm going to give you my point of view which either contradicts what you've just said or completely ignores it."

"I won't take any lessons from you" means "Yes, I may have messed up but you have messed up even more seriously in the past."

In most of these examples the speakers are trying to shift the centre ground of the discussion in their favour.

In the first example, the speaker is inviting the audience to think less of the human cost of putting people out of work and more about the positive side of the redundancies, i.e. greater efficiency, higher profits, lower losses, etc.

The second example converts the money-saving practice of endlessly repeating popular programmes into a positive, i.e. acknowledging we all live busy lives and that sometimes we miss a program we would have wished to see.

The third example is just a rather deceitful device for concealing a future intention in such a way that the speaker can wriggle out of the lie when the intention is implemented, i.e. "We had no plan then, but things change and we have a plan now."

In the fourth example the speaker is politely preparing the ground for a full frontal verbal assault.

The fifth example attempts to establish the speaker (whose mind was made up long ago) as an open-minded listener.

The sixth example shifts attention from the speaker's failure in absolute terms to the world in which we all make mistakes and, relatively speaking, one in which the critic has made worse mistakes than the speaker.

In all these cases, the speaker is defining the scope of the discussion and taking control of the language. Most arguments, and particularly political arguments, draw their energy from the battle to establish the scope of the debate. Most commonly it is about who succeeds in defining "the middle ground."

The Brexit negotiations furnish some rather good examples of defining the scope of the discussion and taking control of the language, most but not all from the Remainers' side of the argument.

The first and blatantly obvious definition of the scope came from the EU which refused to discuss the future trading relationship with the UK until the UK had signed, sealed and delivered a Withdrawal Agreement. This was an absurd stipulation, if only on the grounds that the UK could not know whether it could afford to pay the EU's demands for money before it knew how much damage the EU intended to inflict on the UK economy. It also meant that if the UK accepted this stipulation, it would have to surrender most of its bargaining strengths before any free-trade talks could take place, thus ensuring that the UK would be in a weak bargaining position whenever the free-trade talks eventually started.

Another example of defining the scope was the introduction of the concept of a "hard and soft Brexit." From the Leavers' viewpoint, there was only one Brexit which they defined as "Leaving the EU and taking control of our borders, our laws and our money." This slogan was in itself an attempt by the Brexiteers to define the centre ground of the debate. When the Remainers introduced the soft Brexit option, they shifted the ground away from a clear break with the European Union toward half a break or a quarter of a break or, finally, no break at all. At the start of negotiations, Theresa May attempted to hold to a genuine Brexit, with her famous red lines. But the Remainers were determined to dilute Brexit to the point where there would be no substance to the word. They argued that the UK should remain within the Customs Union (which would mean the UK could not have an independent trading policy). Then some of them argued we should also stay in the Single Market, which would have meant the UK would have to accept the EU's four freedoms. In an extreme soft Brexit, Remainers argued the absurd proposition that the UK should remain tied to the European Union, subject to all its rules, still paying to support the institution but with no say in how the EU was run or what it did. This was clearly a far worse option than staying in the EU, which was, after all, the EU's and the Remainers' real negotiating objective.

The Brexiteers hit back by saying that the Remainers were trying to put the UK in the position of a "vassal state," which gained some traction with the public (at least that part of it which knew what "vassal" meant), but less so with Parliament and the media.

Far more effective was the battle the Remainers fought to repudiate Theresa May's dictum that "No deal was better than a bad deal." Given that this principle is essential in any negotiation, the Remainers' objection to it was inexplicable – or rather explicable only if:

- they had no experience of negotiating, and/or
- they were happy to accept whatever terms the other side deigned to offer.

The Remainers failed to understand that if you "take no deal off the table," as they continually demanded, the negotiation is over. You have nothing to negotiate with.

Toward the end of the negotiation, there was much debate about the possibility of the UK leaving without a deal. This possibility was almost universally described as "crashing out" and the effects as "catastrophic" and "disastrous." While there would no doubt be serious problems with leaving without a deal, especially as it seemed that the UK government was ill-prepared for such an eventuality, the language of "crashing out," "catastrophe," and "disaster" was calculated to close down any serious debate of the possibility. After all, who would seriously consider wilfully causing a "catastrophe." The Remainers firmly occupied the centre ground and those who simply argued that we should leave the EU (in effect, the 17.4 million who had voted to leave) were cast as extremists.

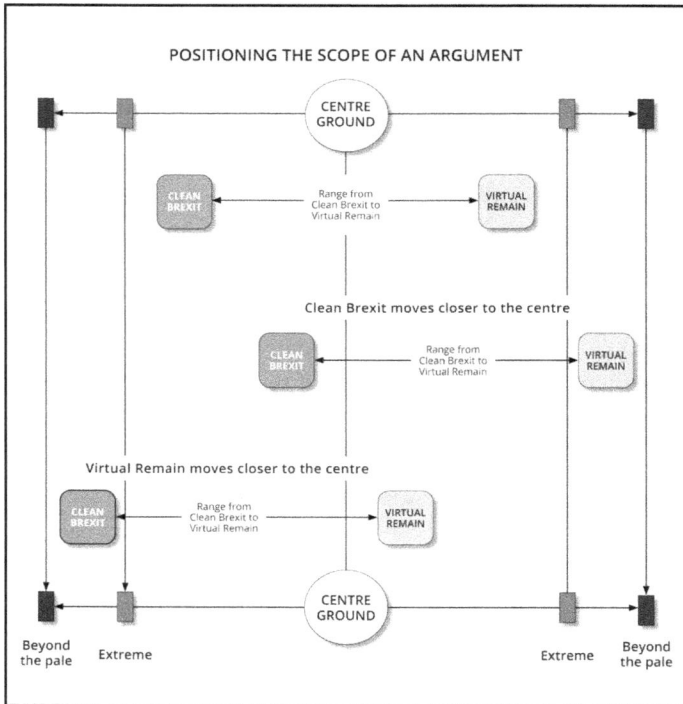

POSITIONING THE SCOPE OF AN ARGUMENT

In the battle within the UK for establishing where the centre ground lay, the Remainers, with the help of the British establishment, were the clear victors, moving Virtual Remain to the centre ground and portraying "clean" Brexit as extreme.

6.3.3 Power distribution

The EU negotiating team did exactly what was expected of them. Their objective was to ensure, if at all possible, that the UK was worse off outside the EU than inside it. This was not because of any anti-British sentiment; it was simply an inevitable outcome of an understanding of the nature of the issue. If we refer to the EU's weaknesses in the negotiation, we find in the list:

> Disconnect in some member states between the Commission (an unelected bureaucracy) and the people.

The EU is a project which is rather (and, in some cases, far) more popular with the political establishment of the member states than it is with their publics. In Italy, a majority of the people are sceptical about the benefits of EU membership. Even in France, which, through the Common Agricultural Policy (CAP) and the status it enjoys within the organisation, benefits greatly from the Union, President Macron has said that if they held a referendum on EU membership, the country would probably vote to leave. Clearly the UK's decision to depart was a serious blow to the project itself, a blow felt most acutely by the EU Commission whose very existence seemed to be threatened by the UK's departure.

It was therefore imperative that the EU Commission made it clear to all other member states that anyone leaving the European Union would have to pay a very high price (literally and metaphorically). So the EU negotiators did exactly what they should have done. They identified those parts of the withdrawal process that:

- would involve the most detailed and time-consuming discussion to give the UK the time to reconsider;

- had nothing to do with the UK's primary negotiating objective.

They insisted that before any discussion of any future trading relationship, there must be a full, legally binding agreement on the terms of the UK's departure.

Following on from their first mistake (the assumption that this was a non-conflict negotiation), the UK negotiators made their second catastrophic mistake when they agreed to the EU's pre-negotiation terms.

Why was this a catastrophic mistake? Because it broke one of the fundamental rules of negotiating, i.e. to focus the negotiation on your own objective. The UK had decided to leave the EU. Essentially what it wanted from the EU was a free-trade deal. Of course, it also wanted good relations with the EU on a bi-lateral (i.e. UK/EU) basis in many areas, but the key to a successful negotiation for the UK was a free-trade deal. So the EU negotiators said they wouldn't even discuss future trading arrangements until the Withdrawal Agreement had been signed. And the UK negotiating team agreed.

What should the UK have done? Any competent negotiator would have said that the negotiations had to cover both the terms of withdrawal **and** the future trading relationship. If the EU had refused for any reason, the UK negotiators should have declared the EU's position unreasonable, terminated negotiations, and said they would prepare to leave unilaterally by the 29th March 2019 deadline on WTO terms. They should have added that, of course, throughout the withdrawal period, their door was open to any approach from the EU on any matters of concern. (Given the demands the EU Commission has made in the Withdrawal Agreement that they drew up with Theresa May, it is clear the EU would have had many matters of concern, primarily how to get the UK to pay tens of billions of pounds in order to leave.)

Instead, the UK agreed to proceed on the basis stipulated by the Commission. Why? Were they forced to accept the Commission's terms? No. They could have walked away and taken two years to prepare for an orderly, managed exit on WTO terms. So why did they do it? Because the UK negotiators misread the nature of the negotiation. They failed to understand it was a conflict negotiation. They adopted a conciliatory approach, apparently believing that by giving the Commission what it wanted at the beginning, they could be sure the Commission would be more reasonable and generous later in the process.

Instead, of course, the EU negotiators logged each concession as a victory and clear evidence that the UK would give in to their every demand. That was a perfectly reasonable conclusion for the Commission to draw from the UK's conduct of the negotiations. No doubt the UK negotiators did their best to win small victories in the interminable grappling with the minutiae of the Withdrawal Agreement but they had little success. If you study the Withdrawal Agreement (some 585 pages), you will find it reads like an EU wish-list rather than a well-balanced, fairly negotiated agreement. It is predominantly about the UK's continuing obligations and how much the UK will still have to pay. There is almost no element of reciprocity. But the failure of the UK negotiators to achieve a balanced Withdrawal Agreement is as nothing compared to their catastrophic error at the very start of the negotiations in allowing themselves to be diverted from their own core objective.

Which brings us to the third mistake made by the UK negotiators. One of our negotiating rules is that you should use your strengths judiciously, reserving them for the attainment of core objectives. But the UK negotiators agreed to pay substantial sums of money to the EU without attaining any of their own objectives. Although not legally obliged to pay anything, or very little, for leaving the EU, they agreed to pay £39 billion. This was a contribution to the running costs of the EU after the UK had left, during a period when the UK would have no say in what the EU was doing or spending. The UK also agreed to pay further billions of pounds for a transition period during which, again, the UK would have no say in the EU's decisions but would still be subject to its law and rules.

Were these concessions necessary? No. Why did the UK make them? We come to the UK negotiators' fourth mistake and to the role of the Remainers.

The Brexit negotiations were unusual in that one of the parties (the UK) was bitterly divided over the objective.

This diagram below shows that, throughout the negotiating process, those who wanted to remain within the EU (the Remainers) continued to press their case directly with the UK government and indirectly with the EU Commission, despite the result of the 2016 referendum.

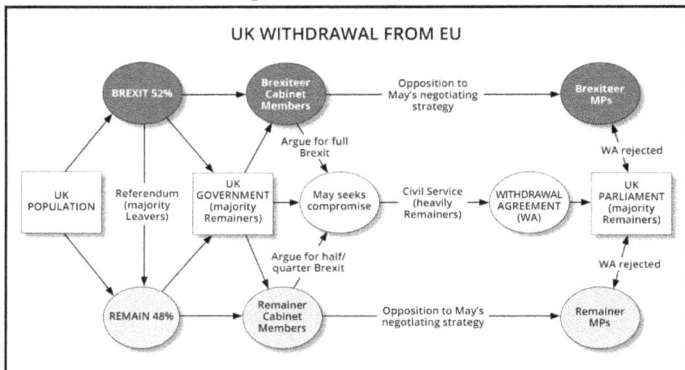

UK WITHDRAWAL FROM EU

As we have stated earlier, to succeed in any negotiation you need to focus on clearly defined objectives. The referendum clearly set an objective, albeit by a relatively small margin, for the UK to leave the EU. Theresa May's government undertook the task of negotiating the UK's departure. But for the UK to succeed in the ensuing negotiations, it was necessary that the whole country (the government, Parliament and people) should unite behind the negotiating team to achieve the best possible terms from the EU.

The opposite happened. From the moment the result was announced, the Remainers undertook to negotiate with the government, effectively on behalf of the EU. They argued that we should show good will to the EU by immediately guaranteeing full rights (which are as good or better in the UK than anywhere in the EU) to all EU citizens living in the UK without making such an offer conditional on reciprocal arrangements for UK citizens living in the EU. Remainers described the requirement for a reciprocal arrangement as blackmail. It was extraordinary that a perfectly reasonable offer, designed to provide UK citizens in the EU with the same protection we were offering EU citizens in the UK, should have been the subject of vitriolic criticism. It was doubly astonishing in that the UK had at least three times as many EU citizens in the UK as the EU had British citizens in the EU, and was therefore making an extremely favourable offer to the EU. After all, the UK has a generous welfare system and the only completely free national health service.

Then the Remainers objected to Theresa May's dictum that "no deal was better than a bad deal," thus ignoring the first principle of negotiating (i.e. if you can't walk away from the table you have no power at all in the negotiation).

If you can never say No, in the end you have to say Yes to whatever you are offered. (See 6.3.3.1 Why you must be able to say No.)

And throughout the negotiations, many Remainers argued for a second referendum to endorse or reject whatever terms the EU finally agreed. Given that the EU wanted the UK to remain within the EU, the possibility of a second referendum gave the EU a powerful incentive (not that one was needed) to offer the UK the worst possible terms (see 6.3.3.2 The idea of a second referendum).

This schism in the UK between the Brexiteers and the Remainers continued throughout the process. As we have previously noted, the UK government then made several egregious negotiating errors, but at the heart of the failure of the UK government to achieve an equitable deal was the determination of the Remainers to keep the UK as a member of the EU in all but name. Remainers argued for UK membership of the Customs Union, thus precluding the UK from making free-trade deals on its own behalf, and for UK membership of the Single Market, thus effectively compelling the UK to accept the EU's four freedoms, despite knowing that the UK would have relinquished any right to contribute to the EU decision-taking process. Clearly the outcome was a deal far worse than staying in the EU, which, as we have noted elsewhere, was precisely what the EU negotiators intended.

In other words, consciously or unconsciously, the Remainers did everything in their power to ensure the UK would be offered the worst possible deal. They were so determined to subvert the outcome of the referendum that they proved a more effective antagonist to Theresa May and the UK negotiating team than the EU Commission itself.

(The moral of this story is self-evident. You cannot hope to succeed in a conflict negotiation if almost half your team is batting for the other side.)

6.3.3.1 Why you must be able to say No.

It's a basic principle in any negotiation that you must be able to walk away. Why this is so is so blindingly obvious that there is no need for an explanation.

Or so I thought.

But I was wrong. When, in a discussion paper on Brexit, I expressed, in passing, my support for Theresa May's dictum that "No deal is better than a bad deal," I was astonished to receive a number of comments querying or contradicting what I had assumed was a self-evident truth.

So in September 2017, I published the following explanation:

> Let's say I want to buy your car. You say you want £6,000 for it. But I've checked Glass's and your car is worth only £4,000. I offer you £2,000. So far we have a normal negotiating situation. The seller wants more than I wish to pay. I wish to pay less than the seller wants. We can now explore a possible compromise (e.g. £4,000).

> But then, inexplicably, before we negotiate, I confess that, whatever happens, I'm going to buy the car anyway (i.e. any deal is worse than no deal.)

> The minimum price I'm going to pay now is £6,000. If the seller is really ruthless, the price is likely to go up. It certainly won't go down because I've said I must buy the car whatever.

> Geddit?

I recount this incident not to enlighten you on the basic principles of negotiating (of which you, like most people, are well aware) but to advise you that it requires enormous effort to overestimate the stupidity of a minority of people, a stupidity matched, if not surpassed, by those UK parliamentarians who, in April 2019, as the Brexit issue reached one of its many climaxes, seized control of Brexit and promptly voted to "take no deal off the table", thus effectively adopting a supine position and inviting the EU to jump all over them, an entirely superfluous invitation, given that the EU had already administered a pretty thorough thrashing in the Withdrawal Agreement.

(Author's apology: That's one long sentence, not entirely consistent with my advocacy of simplicity and brevity!)

6.3.3.2 The idea of a second referendum

While on the detail of the Brexit negotiation, it's worth mentioning a second idiocy that I tried to counter at the same time. This took the form of a demand that whatever the result of the Brexit negotiation, the issue should be subject to a second referendum before it was approved. Again, many people could not understand why this was a bad idea. Again, I explained:

> I want to leave the golf club that my wife and I belong to but the club want us to stay because we pay for a lot of the facilities. I say I'm definitely leaving; the decision is final.
>
> But my wife, who really wants to remain a member, says "Why don't we wait to see how much compensation they're going to demand before we finally decide?"

I explain to my wife, "If you tell them we are going to reconsider our decision to leave on the basis of the terms they offer, obviously **they will offer us the worst possible terms because they want us to stay.**"

She smiles because, being intelligent, she knows this is true but she doesn't care because she wants to remain a member. But then I point out that, given that we really are leaving, all she is doing is ensuring we leave on the worst possible terms – which really isn't very helpful.

6.3.3.3 Footnote

It is of course possible that these two examples of apparent imbecility were in fact a Machiavellian scheme to ensure the EU offered the UK the worst possible deal so that it would be obvious that Brexit should be cancelled. But that would mean the UK Remainers were utterly unscrupulous and undemocratic, a sad indictment of that sizeable proportion of the Remain voters who were unable to accept the result of the referendum.

(In passing, we should point out that democracy is predicated on the assumption that those who are on the losing side accept the will of the majority. The UK Parliament promised to implement the democratic will of the UK people, as expressed in a referendum. In that many Remainers refused to accept the verdict of the referendum, it is fair to say that they have seriously and possibly fatally damaged a key democratic principle. The implications for the UK are profound.)

6.3.4 What you say and what you think

There is another feature of negotiating which the Remainers either didn't understand or chose to ignore. What you say and what you really think are not the same thing. For example, the UK negotiators might have concluded before negotiations began that:

a) it would not be acceptable to leave the EU without a deal

b) any final deal would have to be approved by the UK population

But only someone without even the most tenuous grasp of basic rules of negotiating would have revealed to the EU that this was what the UK really thought. And yet, throughout the negotiations, that is precisely what many Remainers did.

In my example of buying a car, I offer £2,000 for a car which I think is worth £4,000 and which the vendor hopes to sell for £6,000. Now I could say:

> I'm offering you £2,000, but I realise this is a ridiculously low figure and I don't really mean it ... and in any case, I want to make it clear that, regardless of price, I am determined and committed to buying the car.

But no sane person would do that, would they? Yet that is what many of Remainers did. The UK negotiators fought valiantly to hold on to the "No deal is better than a bad deal" mantra, but their position was continually undermined by the Remainers in the UK Parliament who scoffed at the mantra throughout and finally legislated to prevent even the possibility of leaving with no deal.

It has been said that the Brexit negotiations have proved to be the worst humiliation the UK has suffered since Suez. Any serious analysis of the negotiations will reveal that the humiliation was largely self-inflicted.

6.4 THE GOOD DEAL

Enough of Brexit! Let's consider one or two general features of negotiating.

It's been said that a good deal is a deal from which everyone comes away happy. There is some truth in the dictum, but only when all parties have realistic expectations and are seeking compatible outcomes (e.g. buying/selling a car; negotiating a supplier contract). If the objectives of the parties are compatible, and all the parties have realistic expectations, based on their relative strength and weakness, then all can come away satisfied.

In situations where the objectives and hoped-for outcomes of the parties are not compatible (e.g. disputes where both parties lay claim to the same piece of land; where one party seeks precisely the opposite of the other party), a good deal – indeed any deal – is much less likely.

Of course, negotiating is not an exact science. Participants may not have clear objectives; they may not have defined their own red lines; they may not fully understand their own strengths and weaknesses, much less those of the others. In such a situation, those who are well prepared are likely to have the advantage and will probably achieve more from the deal than their actual bargaining strength would seem to justify. And, of course, if the other party is stupid or ill-prepared or incompetent, a shrewd and skilled negotiator may well have a field day.

I should also make the point that negotiating is as much an art as a science, by which I mean that after you have done all the analysis to prepare for the negotiations, you need to employ an open and creative mind. It's a bit like driving a car. You're on a journey. First you need to know where you're going; then you plan a route. You make sure you know how to drive your chosen vehicle and that you have enough fuel to get there. On the way, you may need or want to make a detour. And all the while, you will be using your driving skills to keep you on the road, to set the speed and choose the right gear for the terrain you are passing through. Perhaps it would be possible to describe and explain every adjustment to the steering wheel, every change of gear, but that's not how driving works. We develop a feel for the car and the road – and then we drive, part skill, part instinct and part intuition. It's the same with negotiating.

I was once asked to provide our media coverage analysis service for a major UK exhibition, an exhibition that was likely to attract a great deal of national news media interest. The snag was that the client wanted full reports on the volume and content of the coverage daily, by eight o'clock each morning. This meant that I and some of my staff would have to work through the night. I would have to drive to King's Cross about midnight to pick up the national newspapers, bring them back to the office, ask a skeleton staff to extract, analyse and code the articles, and then prepare a report, run off six copies and drive over to the exhibition to deliver the reports to my clients. (This was before you could access almost every media source through the internet and before you could deliver almost instantaneously reports by email.)

The exhibition was to run for two weeks, so accepting the job was going to put a great deal of strain on a highly motivated, but still small, company with a limited number of trained staff. Given the difficulties, I could have turned the work away, but the sponsor was a valued client and I was loath to refuse.

First, I discussed the project with my employees and asked for volunteers to undertake the night work. We negotiated the money I would need to pay them and I included this amount in my costing. I then added my own time (charged at double my hourly rate because of unsocial hours), the logistical costs, an allowance for the disruption the work would cause to our normal operations – and came up with a figure. In normal circumstances I would simply double the figure to calculate the price.

And then I thought again. I asked myself a series of questions:

- How important was it for the exhibition organisers to be able to measure the success of their operation?
- How much could they afford?
- Who else could do it?

The answer to the first question was clear. It was very important. The costs of the exhibition were spectacular and I knew from my talks with the organisers that they needed to prove, if possible, their competence in running so large a project.

The answer to the second question was open – but whatever I charged would be derisory in the context of the exhibition's budgets.

The answer to the third question was particularly pertinent. We were pioneers in the formal analysis of the reach and effect of new media coverage. To the best of my knowledge, at the time, there was no one else who could do it.

So I concluded that, although we were a very small company with limited resources, and the client was a dominant force in its sector and extremely wealthy, we had the power in this negotiation. There was a temptation to abuse the situation.

On the other hand, the sponsor was a valued client for whom we were providing other media-related services, and I had no wish to alienate them. Instead of using my usual formula to decide the price (i.e. doubling all the direct costs), I decided that on this occasion it was fair to double them once more. I considered going in at an even higher price, so as to allow them to beat me down, but I rejected this ploy. Instead, I sat down with the organisers and explained what we needed to do to fulfil the contract and told them that the price I was offering was non-negotiable because it was fair. They agreed.

I could have done the work for less. And I'm pretty sure I could have charged more. But I was content (although it disrupted my sleep patterns for a couple of weeks). The client was happy because they had someone they trusted to meet their outrageous deadlines. I was happy because the project made a higher profit than usual. And my excellent relationship with the sponsor remained intact because it was clear I had not abused the situation.

Negotiation, part science and part art, is, in the end, a matter of judgement.

7

POLITICS IN BUSINESS

There are no morals in politics; there is only expedience.

Vladimir Lenin

When I left university and took my first "proper" job in the market research department of the Swiss pharmaceutical company, I assumed that we were all there to achieve the corporate goals. I assumed these corporate goals were:

> to use the company's resources to produce products and services that our customers wanted at a price they could afford and which would make enough money after direct costs to cover all overheads, provide shareholders with a profit and the company with enough to invest in its future.

Of course each department had its own departmental goals, but these were all designed to contribute in their own way to the fulfilment of the corporate objectives.

And I recognised that I, as an individual, like all the other employees, had my own goals. But again I assumed that I was employed to contribute to the corporate goals by playing my part in fulfilling departmental goals. It was what I would call a corporate goal-centred world.

I guess I was a little naïve.

The company I worked for was extremely well-managed. It had put in place some highly sophisticated and subtle techniques to keep all employees on the straight and narrow. Job descriptions were clear and coherent. Staff and managers were well trained. There was a career path for every employee who wanted one. The company adopted the grandparent management system whereby once a year, everyone had a free-ranging interview with their boss's boss. This gave every employee an opportunity to speak frankly with a senior manager and, for obvious reasons, it kept every manager on his toes. It seemed to me that all you had to do to succeed was perform the role defined in your job description to the best of your ability.

And to a large extent, that was true. But as time passed and I climbed the management ladder, I noticed a parallel world in which there was a disjunction between individual motivations and corporate objectives. What's more, this parallel world had its own rules, its own criteria of excellence, and its own measures of success.

I had discovered the world of politics in business, a world that exists in every company with which I have had dealings. It's a fascinating, complex world in which reason and emotion rub shoulders; in which personal ambition often takes precedence over the interest of the company; in which personal likes and dislikes, prejudices and preconceptions play an important, sometimes crucial, part in decisions.

Suddenly life became even more interesting. Performing one's official duties as an employee was fairly straightforward – focus on the objectives, work hard, use all one's talents – and success was assured. But this newly discovered parallel world of company politics called for a different skill set. In this world you had to take account of other's sensibilities; you had to be aware of their motivations and real objectives; above all, you had to understand where the power lay.

Of course, being good at one's job is important but on its own it is not enough.

I'll be honest with you. I'm not a political animal. I don't have time for manoeuvring behind the scenes, the subtle manipulation of others, the tailoring of decisions to impress or please others, the scheming to promote oneself and undermine one's rivals. And if I'm honest, I don't have any talent for it. If you are a political animal, I have no advice for you and you probably don't need any. If you do need it, I'm sure you can find it elsewhere.

Here, I am only going to advise those, like me, who prefer to focus on the job, on achieving clearly defined goals as efficiently as possible. And that advice is: Beware!

As you progress up the management ladder, you will find that success depends less and less on competence and more and more on political acumen and general clubbability. You should not be surprised. Most companies are traditional hierarchical structures where the primary activity of those at the top is to protect their own interests and to compete for power. You may have been by far the best salesman, market researcher, marketeer, production manager or accountant the company has ever employed, but as you head for the board, that is almost irrelevant. You now need to acquire and deploy a new skill set.

In the course of providing our media coverage analysis service, I dealt with the boards of many large UK companies. Being a tad judgemental, I couldn't help but assess those I met, using my own criteria of intelligence, perspicacity, and effectiveness. I was surprised by the amazing ability range, from excellent at one end to very poor at the other. Evidently, I was using the wrong criteria since everyone I met had achieved board member status, the weak and bad as well as the strong and good.

What are these criteria?

Well, one is how well you fit. We all like to be with others who are like ourselves, who share the same values, who have the same sort of background. The better you fit, the safer you are.

Another required skill is understanding how power structures work, knowing when to make a stand, or, more commonly, when to defer to those with more power. Such adaptability will stand you in good stead.

A third is to be forever aware of the machinations of your colleagues who, whatever their job titles, will be spending much of their time advancing themselves at the expense of anyone who could impede their progress. You too will have to allocate thought and time to such self-promotion and self-preservation.

A fourth requirement is diligent networking. Networking will extend your reach, increase your awareness of opportunities, and enhance your chances if, despite all your astute manoeuvrings, your current employment turns sour (you are passed over or made redundant).

To me, it's a drag, an irritating distraction from getting the job done. It's probably one of the reasons why I wanted to run my own business. But if you decide to stay employed and climb the management hierarchy, it's important to understand that this is how things are.

A very able friend of mine was made redundant from a good, well-paid, middle-management job at the age of fifty. He found it difficult to find employment. I hired him for a while as a consultant and he did a first-class job. Eventually, he found a position with a charity that paid him far less than he had previously been earning. In terms of management skill and commercial acumen I would have put him in the middle ability range of the board members of major corporations, but such appointments were beyond his reach. He would have fitted in well and he had a fair understanding of how power structures work, but he was not a political animal. He had failed to network sufficiently, and he had spent too much energy on doing his job well and not enough on protecting and promoting his personal brand.

And there are others I have known who have been passed over for promotion in their forties, at least in part because of a lack of political acumen, who have then spent the remaining years of their working lives disappointed, demotivated, and locked into jobs they dislike, simply passing the time until they can afford to take the longed-for retirement.

So if you choose the path of managerial employment, be aware and beware.

8

CLIENT RELATIONS

There is only one boss. The customer. And he can fire everybody in the company from the chairman down, simply by spending his money somewhere else.

Sam Walton, founder of Walmart

8.1 THE CLIENT IS KING

(a) "The customer is always right."
(b) "The biggest problem with running any business is the customers."

You'll hear both sentiments widely expressed. And both are true.

The customer is king because without customers you don't have a business. When I was appointed Marketing Manager in the first company I worked for, I was very young. Someone helpfully pointed out to me that I was actually earning less than one or two of the top salesmen who worked for me. It didn't worry me. They were bringing in more business than any of the other sales people. They were very good at performing a function that is the lifeblood of any company – selling our products and services to our customers – and they deserved what they earned.

On the other hand, let's be honest – customers are often irritating, and sometimes infuriating. Clients for our media analysis service would often set difficult deadlines on a whim. On many occasions, we would prepare a report for a client, meeting an almost impossible deadline, only to discover that a week later the client still hadn't read the report and that it wasn't actually needed for another two weeks.

And quite often the client doesn't know what they want, or, perhaps worst of all, doesn't know enough to judge the quality of the service you and your competitors offer. They will go for the best-known brand on the basis that "No one ever lost their job by retaining IBM." No disrespect to IBM, but that approach is a great pity. The client who goes solely by the brand can end up paying far too much for an average or inferior service.

In providing our media coverage analysis service, we put a vast amount of time and energy into refining the analytical process. Media coverage does not readily lend itself to systematic analysis. After all, it consists of an unceasing flow of content which ranges from straightforward accounts of fact, to witty or satirical critiques of people and organisations. Assessing the impact of such a variety of coverage on the different audiences it reached was challenging. Our product, at the end of the process, was a report, clearly written, illustrated with charts and supported by comprehensive statistical appendices. But its true value lay in the integrity of the analysis that, in the main, clients had no means of assessing.

When, after a couple of years, competitors entered the field, we discovered that while their analyses of coverage was fairly superficial, the general quality and appearance of their reports was outstanding. They used high-quality, glossy paper; their charts were beautifully designed and brightly coloured. We realised we had to up our game. Many clients didn't understand how the coverage was analysed. They simply judged by the look of the report.

So while the customer is always right (i.e. you should aim to give them what they say they want), quite often they can be hopelessly wrong about what they need. In such situations, the supplier has an ethical question to face (see 8.3 What They Want or What They Need below).

8.2 MAKING FRIENDS

It may seem bizarre but it's worth mentioning that not infrequently clients who outsource some of their departmental duties are looking for a friend as much as a service company.

They want someone they will enjoy seeing and spending time with. They want someone they can trust. They want someone they can rely on. They want someone they look forward to meeting and in whom they can confide. In short, they want a friend.

This revelation was thrust upon me one day when we had completed a presentation to a government department based in the Midlands. When the presentation was completed, we answered the questions about the service we offered. The questioner, a middle-aged lady, then asked us if we would be based locally if we won the contract. We said No and explained that we operated from London but would be very happy to drive up to the Midlands once a month to present our reports. She seemed a little disappointed. Then, with disarming frankness, she said: "I was rather hoping we could socialise. Really, I'm looking for a friend." It then struck me that this lady was far from unique. If you are providing a service to a client, the best foundation for a lasting relationship is to replicate all the attributes of a friendship.

8.3 WHAT THEY WANT OR WHAT THEY NEED

Given that the customer is king, you might think that the question, "Should you give clients what they want or what they need?" is entirely unnecessary and irrelevant – and in a way you are right. But it is a question that preoccupied me for much of the time we provided media coverage analysis services, especially in the later years.

I conceived of the service we offered as a way that clients (governments or major corporations) could keep informed of everything the media were saying about them. By rigorously analysing the content and readership of the coverage, we could measure the impact of the coverage on those it reached, and thus its effect on the client's brand. This would give our clients a clear understanding of the image that the media were projecting of them.

We provided this service to the governments of most of the Arabian Gulf states, to almost every department of the UK government and to many UK major corporations, including the BBC, BT, most of the major banks, and a large number of other commercial and charitable institutions. An obvious benefit of the service was that if the client knew what the media were saying about them, they would be better able to communicate their message with and through the media to whomever they identified as their target audience/s.

We defined our own target market as ministers in government and the boards of major corporations. In the beginning, these were the people who became our clients, and with government, there continued to be a good market for the service as I intended it to be. But there was a problem that I should have foreseen. When we sold the service to corporations, most often the board member to whom we were asked to report directly was the Head of Public Relations.

The problem emerged more clearly when the competition arrived. Several of the first few companies that were set up to compete with us were headed by public relations people. Fairly quickly it became clear that while we were analysing and reporting on the totality of a client's coverage, most of our competitors were interested only in the coverage that could be attributed to the efforts of their client's public relations department (i.e. they were tasked with measuring the effectiveness of the client's PR operation).

For me, this was a tragic diminution of my original concept. Most of our clients were major corporations very much in the public eye. They were therefore the subject of intense and often critical media scrutiny. Much of the coverage was media-initiated and had nothing to do with the company's PR department (except when they became engaged in damage limitation exercises after the event). This meant that in many cases, our competitors were analysing less than 10% of the total media coverage of the client and could not in any way claim to be providing "the whole picture."

Worse, it meant that these media evaluation companies were being hired to assess the effectiveness of their own clients, with the inevitable conflicts of interest that arose. After all, why would a PR department pay a media evaluation company to prove that they were involved in only a small proportion of the total coverage of the company (perhaps less than 10%), especially when their input on that 10% was marginal and much of the other 90% of the coverage was negative?

The solution was simple. Ignore the 90% of coverage that was media-initiated (as irrelevant to the efforts of the PR department) and focus on measuring how effective the PR department had been in initiating or responding to the 10% of coverage in which the PR department had been involved. And, of course, resist the inevitable temptation to bias the analysis of that 10% in the client's favour.

What I had conceived as a new, professional analytical service to help clients to manage their corporate reputations and to communicate more effectively through the media with their target audiences had become, to some extent at least, little more than PR for the PR department within the company.

We were happy working for government because, in general, ministries and government departments genuinely wanted the service we offered; and the same was true of commercial companies when we were asked to report to the client's market research department. But when working for PR departments in commercial organisations, we were often conflicted.

I pointed out the problem at a number of meetings of the professional association that I and our first few competitors had formed, but it was clear the tide was against me. They were predominantly PR people and saw the system of media coverage analysis – or media evaluation, as it became known – simply as a way of proving the effectiveness of their clients' PR departments.

Now obviously, as a businessman, I should have gone with the flow, maintaining the "proper" service for our governmental clients but providing the cut-down version for commercial clients. But I didn't. I persisted in providing the "proper" service for all. Gradually, over the years, we lost market share until, after some 25 years, I decided to close the service down, giving notice to our remaining clients.

Why did I do this? Probably because I'm stubborn and I was reluctant to admit that the service I had founded had evolved in ways of which I disapproved. But it was also because I was convinced that the companies we worked for needed the complete service we offered. Surely the board wanted to know how the media as a whole were presenting them to their publics? Surely they could see the folly of ignoring the bulk of coverage? Surely they could see the stupidity of putting their PR department in charge of assessing themselves, albeit via an ostensibly independent agency?

Well, to my surprise, in many cases the answer was No to all three questions. Nevertheless, undeterred, I went my own way, with the inevitable consequences.

Was this a mistake? From a normal commercial point of view, of course it was – and I certainly don't suggest that you should ever wilfully go against what your market clearly wants. In fact, I would recommend the opposite. Find out exactly what your market wants and then do all in your power to provide it.

So why did I do what I did? I confess that I was being self-indulgent. Knowingly and wilfully, I persisted in giving my clients what, in my view, they needed, not what they wanted.

There was only one way it could end. All I can say is that I felt happier following my own path and that this was at the very least an exemplary case of focus, determination, hard work, and bloody-mindedness – and therefore very much another **Decision**.

Could this be seen an example of risk-taking that went wrong? Not really. There was no risk. I knew that if I persisted in working against the trend (i.e. providing the whole picture rather than a partial and often misleading one), we would lose business. I also realised over time that my obsession with improving our analytical techniques had little or no bearing on our commercial success because few clients had any idea how the analysis was performed. But I persisted because I enjoyed the challenge of improving and refining our content analysis program. And, for me, there was the further benefit that I believed in the service we were offering.

It is also important to explain that while maintaining our media coverage analysis service, my company, Panarc International Ltd, had diversified into publishing and into designing and maintaining massive informational websites. As time passed, both of these activities generated substantially more income and profit for my company than media coverage analysis. Had this not been so, as a pragmatist, I would certainly have reviewed my position. (I have principles but I'm not a complete idiot!)

9

INNOVATING

There's a way to do it better. Find it.

Thomas Edison

If you find it easy to come up with creative ideas, it's difficult for you to understand the frustration of those not gifted with this ability. Where do your ideas come from? You don't know. For you, it happens. It seems a bit like magic to you – and even more so to those who can't do it.

Now a degree of creativity is not a prerequisite of success. Focus, determination, hard work, and an organising mind will probably be enough. But the ability to conceive good ideas is a definite advantage. Whether you work for others or yourself, your ability to come up with innovative solutions to problems will be much appreciated and enhance your efficiency and your reputation.

If you are creative, before you congratulate yourself on the ease with which you come up with good, innovative ideas, a word of warning. For you, innovating is easy, but if you fail to follow through, if you fail to apply the techniques and skills recommended in this book, success will elude you. Having a good idea is 10% of a successful project; implementing it is 90%.

What can you do if you don't have creative ideas? Most people have some creativity in them but their mind becomes constricted by routine. You do whatever it is you do in the way it has always been done. After all, the way it has always been done has stood the test of time. So "if it ain't broke, don't fix it."

Really! Well, yes, sometimes. But what about the principle of **bettering** (the habit of making things better – see 2.4). To be successful, we should always be looking for ways to make things better. **Simply looking for ways to make things better creates an opportunity to be creative.** Just identifying a problem and asking the obvious questions can lead us to find innovative answers.

The idea for media coverage analysis came out of my chats with the editor-in-chief of Visnews, the television news agency for which I was the Marketing and Development Manager. With a global network of staffers and stringers, Visnews filmed news around the world and syndicated the news footage to all the world's television broadcasters. I was curious about the editorial process. Given that Visnews sold its news coverage around the world, how did the editor-in-chief determine which news events should be covered and which items of coverage should be supplied to each client?

That was my question. What criteria did Visnews apply? I had noticed that Visnews' syndicated service was heavily skewed to news from the USA, Western Europe, Africa and Australasia. There was much less from the Middle East, the Far East, and Russia. Part of the explanation was the difficulty and cost of acquiring news coverage in some of the less well-represented regions, but the editor-in-chief remained confident that the Visnews news service was pretty well balanced and representative. Given the obvious bias, I asked him how he reached that conclusion. He explained, metaphorically tapping a nostril, that an experienced journalist knows a news story when he sees it and knows which stories should be headlined.

Hmm, I thought to myself. There must be a better way of ensuring impartiality, a way of measuring the balance of editorial judgement. We could easily analyse the origin of news stories by region, and then review the results in the context of, for example, population size, political power and economic strength of each region. What's more, we could classify news stories by their subject matter; we could take out the messages the coverage carried; we could code news stories by whether they were positive or negative; from audience figures, we could even calculate their reach; taken together, we could use these data to estimate the effect of the coverage on its audiences. Visnews itself could benefit from such an analysis (to improve the scope of its coverage; to defend itself against accusations of bias), but any person and any organisation in the news would surely be interested in an objective measurement of the amount, the reach, and the effect of media coverage on their image. The concept for media coverage analysis was born.

So just asking questions about the way things are done can prompt ideas on how to do those things better or to do entirely new things, i.e. innovate.

There's another way you can persuade your brain to think creatively. Throughout most of this book, I've been advocating rational thought (i.e. linear thinking in which each item of thought is connected to the one before and the one after). But there are other ways to think, one of which is inherently creative: **analogical thinking**. Analogical thinking generates metaphors and similes. It enables us to see parallels between unconnected spheres of thought.

I once took part in a creative thinking course. First, the organisers eliminated the normal hierarchy by asking all of us, from the MD to the office cleaner, to play games, some silly, some more demanding. Then they gave us a few problems to solve but they asked us to think analogically. For example, they gave us the problem of how best to clean the windows in a tower block with hundreds of windows. (Men cleaning the windows was expensive, slow, and dangerous.) So I asked myself to identify the essence of the problem and to think of an entirely different situation in which the problem had been solved. The essence of the problem was to clean a large number of sheets of glass quickly, efficiently, and cheaply. I looked around, desperately trying to think of an analogy. Then I realised that, within the group, we were all performing such a task all the time. There were twelve people in the group, so there were twenty-four eyes that needed to be kept clean and clear. How did we do it? We had a liquid supply for each eye and an eyelid to clear away the liquid and any dirt. So I suggested each window should be equipped with a liquid and an eyelid (a wiper), to keep it clean. (I could have thought of a car, with its windscreen wiper, but I didn't; I thought of an eye.) I'm not suggesting it was a brilliant idea, but it was an instance of analogical thinking.

At the same course, the organisers posed another problem. We had a field force of eighty medical representatives (reps) whose job it was to visit GPs and inform them of the efficacy of our ethical pharmaceutical products. In common with all sales forces, monitoring the performance and exercising effective control of sales people out in the field was a problem. You could use sales figures in each rep's territory as a rough indication of performance, but territories varied and, in any case, we were as much concerned with the quality of the rep's presentation to the doctors as we were with sales. So I switched my brain to analogical mode and looked for similar situations in which close supervision of individuals was necessary but difficult. What came to mind was detectives. They are out in the field on their own and, according to all the television films I'd seen, tended to be difficult to manage. How did the police ameliorate the problem? In most cases, each detective had a partner. Each kept an eye on the other. To some extent, each monitored and managed the other. So I suggested that we double the size of our sales territories by putting two adjacent territories together and pairing the reps. We would then base our performance assessment on the total sales in the enlarged territory. That should mean that each rep would police the other. If either slacked, the other would have a word. If either rep was having difficulties, the other would be motivated to help. If either rep was behaving really badly, the other could report him to the regional manager. Not a bad "analogical" idea, or so I thought. It was discussed – but sadly, as far as I know, never implemented.

There's an expression in common use – "thinking outside the box." It's generally considered a good idea but there is little advice on how to do it. My suggestions are:

- Always ask yourself how you can do things better
- Identify problems by asking questions, then look for solutions to the problems
- In looking for innovative ideas, try analogical thinking.

I can't guarantee brilliant innovative ideas but this advice may help.

10
DIVERSIFICATION

*It's always best to have more than one string to
your bow.*

English proverb

If you have started your career or set up a business and have
had some success, don't relax into complacency. Always
keep your mind open to the possibility of diversification.
Some degree of diversification is highly desirable. If you
have only one speciality or offer only one product or service,
you are more vulnerable than if you have two or three other
strings to your bow. "Vulnerable to what?" you ask. Well, if
employed, you are vulnerable to an unexpected redundancy;
if self-employed, you are vulnerable to competitors who
undercut or outperform you, or to a sudden collapse of
the market you are in. (My venture into the health-food
business with fresh royal jelly capsules – see Chapter 3:

Luck – came to an end when a Turkish company introduced a freeze-dried version of our product into the market at a much lower price.)

So whatever your expertise, nurture it and value it because it can be the key to diversification, both personal and corporate.

You will have some skills that relate to the particular studies you have undertaken or jobs you have done. Other skills will be more general and usually transferable. Both the particular and more general skills can present you with opportunities to diversify, to expand your horizons, your career or your business.

If you're good at what you do, very often people who have used your services will ask if you can help them with something else, something probably similar or related but not identical to the service you have been providing for them. If you know that you have the required skills and you're sure you can help them, go ahead. But if you can't, ask yourself what additional skill or resources you would need to be able to help them, now or in future. Winning and retaining clients are essential to any business. If a satisfied client offers you the opportunity to expand your portfolio of services, never dismiss the opportunity out of hand. If your clients think you might be able to help, they are probably right. And there are likely to be others who have similar needs.

Always think about your strengths and your skills. Regularly ask yourself:

How can I make better use of my strengths and skills in what I am doing now?

How can I apply my strengths and skills to diversify my career/business into new areas and/or new businesses?

I'll briefly tell you how I developed my business. At each step, I simply asked these two questions and looked for answers. Perhaps I was a little lucky, but at each stage, simply asking the questions seemed to suggest the answers.

Once I had established our media coverage analysis service, I took stock. It had taken five years to win our first client, but now the concept had been launched, it had at least one outstanding merit. Media coverage never ceases. Even before social media, every day there was a vast volume of new material to be processed and analysed. The need for this service would go on and on. There was a temptation to concentrate on our core service and not remain open to other possibilities.

Our first client was the Ministry of Information of Saudi Arabia, a good start, but not a secure basis on which to build a company. I had no guarantee the first annual contract would be renewed. What could we do?

Our first move was to seek more clients in the Arabian Gulf and we sold the service to the Gulf Cooperation Council, giving us another five governmental clients.

Our second move was to build up business in the UK. Our first UK client was British Gas, quickly followed by BT. This helped to reduce our dependency on our Arabian Gulf clients and mitigated the effect of currency fluctuations (our Gulf contracts were in US dollars or Saudi riyals).

We carried on for a year or two, telling our clients what the media (television, radio and the press) were doing to them. (This was before social media had taken off.) Throughout this period we had the market to ourselves.

Then competition began to emerge, first from an American company and then from UK start-ups. But we still had the edge. We were first in the field and now had a track record. We recruited more staff (coders and analysts) to give ourselves greater capacity. Our list of commercial clients (mainly banks and charities) grew. And then we tapped into a rich vein in the public sector. First, we won the BBC contract. Then we began to work for UK government departments, negotiating annual contracts that were renewed for many years. Everything was going well; our client list and our revenues were growing.

But I had a niggling feeling that we should consider other ways of exploiting our resources. What were our strengths? We understood how to communicate through the media with target audiences. After all, we were spending all our time advising our clients (commercial and governmental) on how the media were portraying them to their publics.

But having told our clients what the media were doing to them, we were leaving it to the client to work out what to say to the media, how to respond to the media coverage.

So as a second step we decided to enhance our reports by analysing the issues that preoccupied the media and providing advice on how the client should respond. The "Conclusions" and "Recommendations" sections of our report were expanded to the point where they were regularly submitted to the boards of companies and ministers in government departments. Our reports became in effect consultancy reports based on a professional analysis of the issues, as identified by intense media interest. (For ten years we provided the Department of Works and Pensions, as it was then, with monthly reports – from the time when Tony Blair instructed Frank Field to "think the unthinkable" about welfare reform.)

So far we had concentrated on improving and enhancing our media coverage analysis service, but if we returned to a consideration of our strengths, there were other, more diversified, possibilities we could consider. Since we knew how to communicate to and through the media, perhaps we should consider providing a communications service ourselves. Surely we could offer to communicate our clients' information to our clients' target audiences?

If that sounds as though we were thinking of going into the public relations business, I've misled you. No, what I had in mind was providing an information service to address the problem about which ironically everyone complains – i.e. too much information. I was interested in the idea of organising vast amounts of data into comprehensible, manageable, and navigable units, tailored to the interests of each user.

I discussed the possibility with our oldest client, the Ministry of Information in Saudi Arabia. The minister saw immediately that, with our help, the Ministry could have the means of making available all its general information, all its news releases and up-to-date information about government policies to a vast English-speaking audience which, hitherto, it had found difficult to reach.

The internet had recently been born, and because of our work on the software for our current service, we were up to speed on using computers to organise and present data. And because of our media coverage analysis work for the Saudi Ministry of Information, we already had a large database of information on every aspect of the Kingdom's development.

I set about designing a website and asked my programmer, Stephen Arnold, to write an application that would insert information from our MS Access database into our newly developed website. Within months, we launched the Saudi

Arabian Information website. It had a unique feature (probably unique even to this day) – every email sent to the website was answered the same day.

We now had a valuable and ever-growing information resource, with facts, figures, and slides on every aspect of the Kingdom. What more could we do to exploit this resource?

Every year, millions of Muslims converge on the Holy City of Makkah to perform Hajj, and every year, there is an insatiable appetite for information about the Hajj (the rituals, the travel arrangements, what is expected of the pilgrims, etc.). Here was a subject that lent itself to internet treatment. With the help of various Saudi ministries, we gathered all the relevant information and, on behalf of the Saudi Ministry of Hajj, Panarc set up the first English language website on the pilgrimage to Makkah. We managed the website for five years and attracted millions of visitors.

What else could we do?

We could become a publisher. It was an obvious step. We were publishing information on the websites. Why not use our databases to produce books and booklets to meet the Ministry of Information's needs. Official biographies of the public lives of Saudi kings, booklets on different aspects of the Kingdom's development plans, even advertisements for the Saudi National Day, followed. We were now involved in research, writing, website creation and management, book design, printing, distribution and translation (because of the need for foreign language versions) – as well as supplying our core service of media coverage analysis.

We had become specialists in the analysis and communication of information through a variety of media, through a variety of distribution channels, to a variety of audiences.

I have condensed a business career of thirty years into a couple of pages, so it probably sounds a bit glib, a bit obvious, and even a bit easy. It wasn't. It was very hard work at every stage. We had to face fierce competition in media coverage analysis. We had to adapt to changing circumstances and new technologies. We had to demonstrate commitment and professionalism to our clients in every activity in which we engaged. We won clients and we lost clients. We had times when cash flow problems (i.e. slow payers) forced us to dip into our own personal savings to pay staff. We had to deal with currency fluctuations. And, as noted elsewhere, we had a few problems in managing the money we made. But we kept ahead of the game by regularly asking those two questions:

- How could we make better use of our strengths and skills in what we are doing now?
- How can we apply our strengths and skills to diversify our career/business into new areas and/or new businesses?

If you keep a look out for opportunities, they will find you.

11

USING PROFESSIONALS

There are more fools than knaves in the world, else the knaves would not have enough to live upon.

Samuel Butler

As your career progresses and your personal affairs become more complicated (and, in all probability, as your wealth increases), you will find that you need to employ the services of one or more professionals (accountants, architects, doctors, engineers, financial advisers, surgeons, surveyors).

All these people will have passed the exams that entitle them to claim membership of their profession. The theory is that they are all thoroughly competent at what they do. You don't need to enquire whether the one you are thinking of using is any good. If he belongs to a profession, you can be sure you are in safe hands.

This is, of course, complete rubbish. There are good accountants, architects, doctors, engineers, financial advisers, surgeons and surveyors, and there are bad ones.

If you are blessed with a family that has already established a network of trusted, competent professionals, you will have less of a problem. Even better, if you have members of all the professions in your extended family, you are probably home free! But if, like me, your parents were not so connected, you have to take your chances.

My experience with professionals has not been entirely happy. I have used an accountant who justified his exorbitant charges by explaining that he charged on a standard hourly fee based on a "time spent" basis and since he used untrained and unpaid interns, obviously work on our accounts took a great deal of time. I retained an architect who couldn't be trusted to take accurate measurements and who produced and recommended structurally unsound designs. I have used solicitors who made so many mistakes and were so careless that one almost suspected they were working for the other party. I have been treated by doctors whose handiwork has necessitated an emergency recall to hospital to put things right. And I describe my even less happy experiences with financial advisers elsewhere.

On the other hand, and to be fair, I have retained one firm of excellent accountants, two outstandingly good lawyers, a couple of amazingly good doctors and even one honest financial adviser. I use a rule of thumb when considering professionals. It's **the "one, four, five" rule**. For every ten members of a profession, one will be excellent, four will be somewhere between competent and good, and five will be below average down to bad. I offer this rule as an antidote to the widespread misconception that if you retain a member of a profession, all of them will be competent and worth the money you will be paying them.

How can there be such variation in the professionalism of professionals, all of whom hold the necessary professional qualifications? There are two explanations. First, professionals are people and people make mistakes. All of us make mistakes, but when we hire a professional, we do so in order to avoid the mistakes we fear we would make without their help. When they fail, we are understandably and justifiably disappointed, but we shouldn't be surprised.

The second reason is lack of social mobility. All the professions require people of above average intelligence. Most professionals come from the middle class. (It's not a closed shop, but it is, to a large extent, a closed class.) Like all the social classes, the middle class has its fair share of the clever, the average and the less intellectually gifted. Sadly, this means that some of those who enter the professions are really not up to it. With more and more young people going to university, we can be hopeful that bright kids from less privileged backgrounds will aspire to join the professions. If they do, they will certainly raise the general level of professional performance. But there are many barriers they will have to overcome, not least the limitations that their class origins impose upon them and, in many cases, the limited aspirations of their family and friends.

So in retaining professionals, what should you do? Well, first of all, keep in the forefront of your mind that you are paying. However eminent, or impressive, or pompous the professional you use may be, remember that you are the client and you will be paying their indisputably formidable fees. You know it and they know it. Then:

- checks their CVs
- canvas the opinions of friends and relatives who have used their services
- tactfully ask another member of the profession for any recommendation they will give

None of these selection techniques is foolproof.

Some of those most highly qualified are not necessarily the best practitioners. We recently had a problem with one of our properties, a bungalow in a close in Iver. To the outrage of all but one of those living in the close, a developer claimed to have found a way to open up the end of the close in order to access land on which he could then build one or more houses. My wife and I carefully researched the law and discovered that since the developer had already been given planning permission (despite the objections of the residents of the close, the parish council and the Highways Authority), there was almost no chance of preventing this unwelcome development. We informed the residents of the close of our findings. Unpersuaded, they clubbed together and sought the advice of one of the most eminent lawyers in the country. He told them that they had every chance of stopping the developer in his tracks. The other householders formed a management company and instructed solicitors. Within a few months, despite considerable solicitors' fees, the first new house was built and the foundations for a second had been laid. Clearly the eminent lawyer's advice had, at the very least, erred on the side of optimism.

Canvassing your friends is probably the best bet, except you may well not have any friends with relevant experience, and even if they have, they may not have found anyone they could recommend.

Fellow professionals are extraordinarily wary of suggesting any one professional is better than another. (After all, they have to protect the reputation of the profession as a whole and the assertion of uniform excellence is seen as the primary defence.) But this approach, like the other two, is worth trying. When looking for a surgeon to operate on my knee, I asked one of the nurses in the hospital who was the best.

"Of course, they're all very good," she replied.

I waited. "But …?" I prompted.

Then she gave me a name.

12
MANAGING MONEY

*A wise person should have money in their
head, but not in their heart.*

Jonathan Swift

If you've followed the advice in this book, you are a success.
That means that unless your life goal was essentially altruistic,
you will inevitably have acquired some wealth. In this section
I can give you the benefit of hard-won experience.

I can honestly say that, in this area, my wife and I have
made as many mistakes as anyone. And most of these
mistakes have ensued from a failure to grasp the essential
nature of the financial sector of our economy.

The first and most important truth I am about to reveal,
a truth that, if fully grasped, will protect you and your
money throughout life, is brutally simple. It comes in two
parts. It is this:

The only way the financial services sector can make money is by making money out of your money.

In any relationship where two people have an interest in the same sum of money, each party will give precedence to their own interests.

12.1 INDEPENDENT FINANCIAL ADVISERS

I will tell you how to become rich. Close the doors. Be fearful when others are greedy. Be greedy when others are fearful.

Warren Buffet

Until recently, most Independent Financial Advisers (IFAs) worked on hidden commissions, i.e. money they were paid by financial institutions to hand your money over to these same financial institutions.[3] These hidden commissions, paid by the financial institution to your financial adviser, often represented a substantial bite out of the money which you thought you had invested. This system of remuneration constituted an institutionalised conflict of interest, i.e. would the IFA place your money (a) where you were likely to get the best return or (b) where the IFA was certain to make the highest level of commission?

My first investment, in the early 1980s, was £10,000 put into an investment scheme on which the IFA informed

---

[3] I think it's fair to describe the commissions as hidden because over many years I tried to get a number of IFAs to be honest about their commissions and, believe me, it was like getting blood (mine, of course) out of a stone. More recently, the government has forced Financial Advisers to be more open about their charges and to declare their fees but in my experience they remain peculiarly coy when you demand the complete picture.

us he was taking a modest 2% commission. Imagine my surprise when I received confirmation the money had been placed and the value of our investment was listed as £6,000. What, I asked the IFA, had happened to the other £4,000. That, he brazenly replied, was his 2% commission. It was assumed we would continue to deposit £10,000 a year for the next couple of decades, so the financial institution had paid him all his future putative annual commissions up front out of our initial deposit. But we hadn't agreed to make any further deposits. We couldn't, because as we ran a small, recently established business we had no guarantee of future income. "That's OK," he said cheerfully, "you're not under any obligation to make further deposits, but if you do, rest assured the commission on them has already been paid."

The next scheme we were persuaded to invest in was a government-backed development scheme of student accommodation to be built and rented out over a period of five years. We stood to gain from the tax incentive, the rents and any capital appreciation of the property. Wary of any advice from any IFA, we asked if there was any risk. "None at all," was the reply. "The company guarantees to buy your share in the enterprise at the end of the five years at the market rate or to refund your investment in full, whichever is higher. You cannot lose."

As the scheme was government-backed, we purchased a £10,000 stake, which cost us only £6,000 because of tax relief. At the end of five years, we thought we would at least receive £10,000 but hoped for more, given the increase in property value and the rent that had been paid. Sadly, no. Two weeks before the end of the five years, the company went bust. We were lucky – we got £6,000 back. We had lost five years interest, but it could have been worse.

I challenged the IFA. What about the "You can't lose" promise? The financial adviser adopted the tone of someone addressing a child incapable of grasping the simplest and most obvious of financial truths. "Yes, I told you that you were 100% protected, but of course everyone knows that a company can go bust."

That's just a couple of examples of how you can be duped. In both cases the IFA was, in my view, dishonest.

Now I'm not suggesting all IFAs are dishonest, but I am saying that as they make money out of your money, you should understand that the relationship will conform to the general rules of human nature, i.e. in any relationship where two people have an interest in the same sum of money, each of the parties will give precedence to their own interests.

I've no doubt all IFAs will be outraged by such a suggestion, but based on personal experience, I am convinced I'm right. Let me explain. Your IFA agrees to manage your portfolio of shares. Implicit, if not explicit, in his offer is the claim that he knows how to look after your shares better than you. For his service he will charge anything between 0.5% and 1.5% per annum, depending on the size of your portfolio. So he is guaranteed compensation for his work (his administrative work and his financial expertise).

If you have a portfolio of £1 million and he charges you 1% p.a., you will be paying him £10,000 p.a. He will now place your money/shares on the market as he sees fit. If the shares increase by 10% to £1.1 million, your IFA will get 1% of £1.1 million (i.e. £11,000). Unless there are other charges, you will have made £89,000 gross. Not bad! If inflation is running at 2.5%, you will have made £61,775, or 6.2% in real terms (Row A in the table below).

But if he places your money and he loses 10%, your financial adviser will get 1% of £900,000 (i.e. £9,000). Unless there are additional charges you will have lost a total of 109,000 (the £100,000 fall in the value of your shares and the financial adviser's £9,000 commission), leaving you with £891,000 gross. If inflation is running at 2.5%, in real terms you will have lost a further £22,275, leaving you with £868,725. Your total loss will be £131,275 or 13.1% (Row B in the table below).

Are you beginning to get the picture? Shares go up 10%: you gain £89,000 before taking inflation into account; your IFA takes £11,000. Shares go down 10%: you lose £109,000 before taking inflation into account; your IFA still takes £9,000.

Below you can see the situation for the client if the gain or loss is less – say 5% (Rows C, D, G and H), or if the IFA takes a higher annual fee of, say, 1.5% (Rows E, F, G and H).

	Cap.	% +/-	Gross Value (GV)	IFA %	IFA Comm.	GV-IFA Comm.	Infl.	Capital remaining	Total £ +/-	% +/-
A	£1m	10	£1,100,000	1	£11,000	£1,089,000	2.5	£1,061,775	£ 61,775	6.2
B	£1m	-10	£ 900,000	1	£ 9,000	£ 891,000	2.5	£ 868,725	-£131,275	-13.1
C	£1m	5	£1,050,000	1	£10,500	£1,039,500	2.5	£1,013,513	£ 13,513	1.4
D	£1m	-5	£ 950,000	1	£ 9,500	£ 940,500	2.5	£ 916,988	-£ 83,013	-8.3
E	£1m	10	£1,100,000	1.5	£16,500	£1,083,500	2.5	£1,056,413	£ 56,413	5.6
F	£1m	-10	£ 900,000	1.5	£13,500	£ 886,500	2.5	£ 864,338	-£135,663	-13.6
G	£1m	5	£1,050,000	1.5	£15,750	£1,034,250	2.5	£1,008,394	£ 8,394	0.8
H	£1m	-5	£ 950,000	1.5	£14,250	£ 935,750	2.5	£ 912,356	-£ 87,644	-8.8

It would seem that the system is very much in the IFA's favour.

"Wait a minute!" you say. "I'm paying the financial adviser for his financial expertise. It's much more likely that, with his help, my shares will do better than I could hope to do on my own."

Really! Then why is it very few financial advisers, after taking their fees, can match the tracker funds that simply follow an index of categories of shares?

The truth is this: if we exclude insider trading (which is illegal), buying shares on the stock market is a form of gambling. Using a financial adviser to manage your portfolio is inviting someone to gamble with your money on the basis that if he wins, he takes a share of your money; and if he loses, he still takes a share of your money, but just a bit less.

I have offered many financial advisers a deal. No percentage commission, no fees, but 50% of everything they make above the rate of inflation, and they carry 50% of any losses. They all refused. So I made the offer even more attractive. I removed the penalty if the shares fell in value. Even then they said no. But if they are not confident they can make money above the rate of inflation, why should I entrust them with my money? Why shouldn't I put the money in a tracker fund or eliminate all risk and put the money on deposit where I can earn interest which will at least mitigate the adverse effects of inflation.

Let me hasten to add that there is a genuine and necessary role for financial advisers. The terms and conditions of many financial instruments are complicated. The government's own rules of investment and tax are so arcane that I sometimes suspect they are in a conspiracy with the financial services sector to fleece the public. So we all need help in filling in the forms and conforming to the law. Those who are expert in this field undoubtedly deserve to be paid fairly for their services. My main gripe is about what is fair.

As for their claim that they can handle your wealth better than you, I accept there is some truth in what they say (especially if you are financially ignorant), but again, in my experience, whatever they save you is more than cancelled out by the fees they charge you. So what should you do?

Inform yourself of the basic forms of investment and the degree of risk involved. Identify those forms of investment that you can easily handle yourself (e.g. interest-bearing accounts, investment in unit trusts, index-tracking funds) without incurring the costs of an adviser.

If you decide you need to use a financial adviser:

- Check the reputation and qualifications of any IFA you consider using. IFAs are regulated by the Financial Conduct Authority (FCA) and must have a Certificate in Financial Planning (CERT FP) to register with the FCA.
- Make sure you understand what the financial adviser is telling you. Don't be afraid to ask questions. It's your money (at least, it is until you agree to give him some of it).
- Always insist on full disclosure in writing of the costs to you of any investment (good luck with that!) before taking a decision.
- Make sure that you have written/documentary evidence in support of any promises or guarantees you have been given.

- Finally, understand the essential nature of the relationship between a financial adviser and the client. The client pays the financial adviser some of his money to look after the rest of his money. All the money involved comes from the client; all the risk involved comes back to the client. Whether the client's wealth is increased or decreased, the financial adviser still gets paid.

The daughter of a friend applied to an investment bank for a job. She was the only female applicant. All the candidates were given a sum of money and invited to play the stock market. Presumably the exercise was intended to assess their judgement and their nerves. At the end of the exercise, our friend's daughter had done tolerably well. Some of the men had done brilliantly. They had taken risks that had come off. Others had taken risks and had lost everything and were in debt.

After the exercise, our friend's daughter suggested that all the applicants should put £50 into a kitty and repeat the exercise, but this time play for real. Some of the men declined the invitation. Those who accepted showed at least as much caution as our friend's daughter had in the original test. The moral of this anecdote is simple:

Beware when you let other people gamble with your money.

Incidentally, our friend's daughter, although blessed with a first-class brain, was told that trading on the stock market was not for her. Only the successful, reckless candidates were hired.

12.2 BANKS

Neither a borrower nor a lender be,
For loan oft loses both itself and friend,
And borrowing dulls the edge of husbandry.

Hamlet, Shakespeare

Banks are very keen on projecting an image of themselves as wise and wholly benign institutions who are there for us at every stage of our lives to help us with sage advice and fair, if not generous, access to their money (for mortgages, credit cards and other loans).

In more recent times, this image has taken a bit of a knocking as, one after another, many of the world's great banking institutions have been found guilty of fraud and other dishonest practices (including money laundering) that make Fagin appear a model of financial probity.

So let's get a couple of things straight. The banks are not benevolent institutions, committed to social good; they are powerful organisations whose lifeblood is the money they take out of other people's money. And that's the second point. They don't make anything. They don't create anything. They don't produce anything. In essence, they survive by appropriating some of the wealth of those who do make and create and produce.

I fully recognise that banks are essential. They facilitate the flow of money from savers to borrowers, from investors to wealth creators. They play a crucial role in maintaining the health of a modern economy. But it is clear that in a globalised world they have succumbed to the temptation of avarice, with fairly disastrous consequences for society. By lending irresponsibly, they have created a lumpen population that through mortgages and credit cards is heavily, and for the most part, permanently in debt. A high proportion of most people's income is now spent in paying interest on money they couldn't really afford to borrow. So what should you do?

Never borrow unless you have to.

I have only ever borrowed to buy property. And after borrowing to buy my first two properties (a flat, and then a house in London), from then on I've paid cash for any property I've bought. I use credit cards for daily expenses, but every month I pay off the full amount owed. For the last four decades of my life I have not paid a penny of interest.

Yes, this philosophy does involve some degree of deferred gratification. If I want something but can't afford to pay for it, I don't borrow. I save until I can buy it. I realise this attitude will grate with many today, especially the younger generation who have been trained by the banks, our consumer society, and latterly the government to accept debt as a normal part of life. But I appeal to everyone to grasp how debt and interest work. Even at relatively low interest rates, the average mortgage holder, by the end of the mortgage, will have paid back twice what was borrowed. The providers of credit cards boast that they only charge 20% – 25% p.a. interest on credit card debt while paying the people who provide the money they lend a mere 1% of interest on their deposits.

I should mention in passing that the whole world seems to have become addicted to debt. It's not only people who borrow more than they can afford – in some cases, more than they can ever repay. Governments are at least as profligate. At the time of writing, the USA's total national debt stood at $21.97 trillion (i.e. $29,700,000,000,000) and Italy's national debt stood at almost 132% of GDP.

There are other features of UK banking of which you should be aware. First, they tend to take a short-term view. This short-termist culture is caused by the high financial rewards that bankers get for achieving short-term results. It has the unfortunate consequence of starving industry of the long-term loans necessary for long-term investment.

A second feature, in part another result of short-termism, is that UK banks tend to be keen to lend you money when you don't need it but are far less enthusiastic when you do. I was lucky in that I didn't have to borrow money to set up my media coverage analysis service, but businesses requiring substantial capital investment have no choice but to go to the banks. They are then likely to find they have to provide some security for the loan (e.g. a lien on their home) and to face heavy and sometimes crippling interest rates and terms.

After my media coverage analysis business began to make money, the manager of my company's bank took me out to lunch. "I'd be happy to lend you £200,000," he said during lunch. I was surprised. "I don't need £200,000," I replied. He was disappointed. "You could buy some local warehousing," he suggested. (There were a number of storage buildings in the area.) I looked at him blankly. "For what?" I asked. Clearly he didn't understand my business. He was solely concerned with selling me money, encouraging me to diversify into a field about which I (and I suspect he) knew nothing.

When dealing with banks, always remember you are the customer. Try to make sure you are using them; try to make sure they are not using you. Just remember:

In any relationship where two people have an interest in the same sum of money, each party will give precedence to their own interests.

12.3 SAVING

Money is a terrible master but an excellent servant.

P.T. Barnum

I'd like to give an unequivocal blessing to the habit of saving. And I will. Saving is good because it means you have some control of your fate and your life. So save as much as you can. That's my advice.

But I have to recognise the tide of opinion is against me. In the last ten years the most significant aspect of government economic policy has not been "austerity." It has been a massive transfer of money from savers to borrowers. Interest rates for savers have been kept low, so low that there has even been talk of negative interest rates. Low interest rates have been necessary to protect borrowers from financial ruin and, particularly, to save those with mortgages from negative equity. But to save borrowers from financial disaster, governments had to find the trillions needed from somewhere – which, of course, meant those with money, i.e. savers.

While those in work have complained that their income has stagnated, those on fixed incomes derived from interest on savings have seen their income halved or quartered. Borrowing has been unusually cheap, encouraging people to borrow and spend rather than to save.

So the government seems determined to favour borrowers and spenders over savers; and the banks are only too happy to welcome more and more of their citizens into a lifetime of bondage.

No one can foretell the future with any certainty, but I suspect it will not end well. In the meantime, despite low interest on savings, save; don't borrow. Save not to earn the currently derisory levels of interest but simply to assert your freedom from the shackles of debt. And, of course, don't borrow (except to buy a potentially appreciating asset), if you want to avoid spending a substantial proportion of your income on interest repayments.

12.4 PROPERTY

> *Real estate cannot be lost or stolen, nor can it be carried away. Purchased with common sense, paid for in full, and managed with reasonable care, it is about the safest investment in the world.*
>
> Franklin D. Roosevelt

With any investment, past performance is no guarantee of future performance. That said, property is probably the best of all long-term investments.

Why?

Well first of all, you need somewhere to live. You can either pay rent, which has some advantages (e.g. few responsibilities), but the money you pay in rent is gone for ever. Or you can buy. There are times when it is relatively easy to buy, and times when it is much more difficult. But easy or difficult, do it. Yes, you will almost certainly have to borrow. And that means that until you pay off the mortgage you will be in debt to the bank and paying a substantial part of your income in interest. But even so, in this particular case it is worth it.

Why is it worth it? Because:

- your flat or house is an appreciating asset. You buy a new car, and as you leave the forecourt of the vendor, thousands of pounds fall away from your net wealth. Of course, you have the pleasure of owning a new car, but it's scarcely a good investment. A house, on the other hand, is.

- you will need a surveyor and a solicitor to purchase the property, but these are one-off costs. You won't need to pay a financial institution and, possibly, a financial adviser year after year to look after your investment.

- assuming you buy a house freehold, you own the house and the land on which it stands. Whatever happens, you own an asset that is real. You put money in a bank; the bank can go bust. You buy shares; you can lose all your money. Unless you live in a flood, hurricane, or war zone, your house will be there for you in good times and in bad.

- you can make an unlimited capital gain on your house (assuming it is your main place of residence) without paying any capital gains tax when you sell it.

- a house is an asset, probably increasing in value, that you need and enjoy every day.

Of course the law and the tax regime may change. Already the government is looking with a predatory eye on the property market. It has imposed stamp duty at such a high rate that it is now generating a considerable amount of money for HMRC. Nevertheless, as things stand, property should form a substantial part of your wealth portfolio. So here's what to do:

- Build up a deposit (by saving, or by borrowing from the bank of Mum and Dad, or by inheriting the money).
- Buy a flat or house.
- Pay off the mortgage as quickly as you can manage.

12.5 INTEREST – FRIEND AND FOE

> *Compound interest is the eighth wonder of the world. He who understands it, earns it … he who doesn't … pays it.*
>
> Albert Einstein

Most of us will be both borrowers and lenders during the course of our lives.

Even those of us who hate borrowing will almost certainly have to borrow to purchase our first property. And today, after years of indoctrination, many have become inured, through access to easy credit, to borrowing as an essential part of life.

It is also true that most of us will, at some time, be involved in saving, if only as part of provision for a pension.

It is therefore crucially important to understand a common feature to both borrowing and lending, i.e. interest. Interest is what you pay for the privilege of borrowing and what you earn as your reward for lending.

MORTGAGES: In this section on managing money I have advised you to borrow as little as possible for as short a time as possible. Here's why.

Let's say you borrow £100,000 as a mortgage at 3% p.a. and you agree to repay at the rate of £400 a month, or £4,800 p.a. (Repayment Plan One).

What's the situation after twenty years? Well, you will have paid £96,000 (20 x £4,800), against the £100,000 you borrowed. But of that £96,000, **£47,633 will be the interest you have paid.** You will have paid off only £48,367 of the debt, which means you still owe £51,633.

Now let's keep everything the same, except that you pay £800 per month, or £9,600 p.a. (Repayment Plan Two). Around **April of Year 13**, your mortgage is completely cleared and you will have paid a mere (!) **£21,600 in interest.**

That's why you should borrow as little as possible and pay it back as quickly as possible. (See Appendix C for a spreadsheet showing the figures over the years.)

CREDIT CARDS: As for credit cards, don't ever fail to pay them off each month. The average credit card debt is around £3,000. The average interest on credit card debt is 19% p.a. If you run an average debt on your credit card of £3,000 for ten years, you will have paid £5,700 pounds in interest for the privilege. You would have to be mad to agree to such a deal. (Sadly, such madness is rife!)

If you were really crazy, and instead of holding your running debt at £3,000, you used a combination of credit cards and increased you credit card debt by £3,000 each year, at the end of ten years, you would owe more than £88,000 (i.e. roughly double your average borrowings during the ten-year period).

NB: I've ignored the stipulation that you have to pay off a minimum amount each month on credit cards because despite these modest repayments, you can still (a) maintain an average debt level and (b) increase your debt level as supposed above.

SAVING: Just as the interest you pay on borrowing mounts up with alarming speed, so the compound interest you can earn on savings can produce similarly surprising but happier effects. We live in a period of low interest rates, but even so, compound interest can become your friend. £10,000 invested at 5% compound interest for ten years will be worth more than £16,300 at the end of the tenth year.

IF ONLY: If only the banks paid savers what they charge credit card borrowers. If the banks paid savers 19% and you deposited £10,000 with them, after ten years your deposit would be worth just under £57,000. (Sadly, no chance!)

13
MANAGING YOUR PERSONAL BRAND

Thus is man that great and true Amphibium, whose nature is disposed to live not only like other creatures in diverse elements, but in divided and distinguished worlds.

Religio Medici, Sir Thomas Browne

(I've put this section in but I have to confess my heart isn't in it. I'll explain why at the end.)

Throughout your career you will be projecting an image of yourself. Yes, you know what you are, or I hope you do. (You did agree to be honest with yourself on page one of this book.)

But how do others see you? They don't have access to the inner workings of your mind, so their knowledge of what you are has to be inferred from:

- what you say
- what you do
- what you look like

It is not possible to give a checklist of what you should say, do, and look like in order to create what you think is the right image of yourself. It depends on many variables (what you actually are; what image you wish to project; whom you're with; what preconceptions they have; what stereotypes they apply to you, etc.), but I can say with certainty:

- they will have an image of you
- you can usefully look on that image as your brand

What you say is your most powerful and refined method of developing your brand. Your words, the grammatical structure of your sentences, the manner of your delivery, and your accent will all be powerful indicators to your audience of the type of person you are. The problem with words is that they lend themselves to deceit. The consummate self-projectionist, like the conman (not, of course, you in either case) will be adept in creating false impressions.

In that respect, what you do is a more solid base for brand-building. It's true that actions can be misinterpreted, but in the main, what you do is likely to be seen as an excellent indicator of the person you are.

As for what you look like, I can say that your physical appearance, how you dress, and how you handle yourself, is likely to have an immediate, powerful, and often enduring effect on how others see you. In general, **you should wear whatever is expected of someone in the position to which you aspire.**

The problem with managing your personal brand is that just as others don't have access to the inner workings of your mind, you don't have access to the inner workings of theirs.

O wad some Power the giftie gie us
To see oursels as ithers see us.

Robert Burns

You can ask others to tell you. But it's embarrassing to ask, and you can never be sure that the respondent is being honest. That said, it is still worth doing from time to time. Pick someone whose judgement you respect, who has no personal axe to grind and who, if they had an axe, would not be tempted to bury it in your head. When they give you their answer, you won't necessarily be any closer to the truth about your image, but how they judge you and on what criteria will almost certainly surprise you.

"I've always thought of myself as extremely empathic," says someone with the people- handling skills of Genghis Khan suffering from a severe migraine. "I've never thought of myself as particularly accommodating," says someone in the final and terminal stages of sycophancy. "I'm pretty sure I'm not primarily motivated by money," says someone who, when a well-liked work colleague is leaving after many years of faithful service, always writes the biggest farewell message in prime position in the staff card and then, sadly, finds he has no spare change in his pocket to contribute to the leaving gift.

Why did I say I feel ill at ease in writing this section? It's because I have never followed the advice I am giving here. That doesn't mean I don't believe what I've written. I do. I know that in all situations, people observe each other and form judgements. And just as you need to know the rules in any game, so those who know the rules of self-projection have the best chance of impressing their peers and superiors, which seems to be the primary goal of personal branding.

Indeed, whole books have been dedicated to this subject, claiming that personal brand management can be the whole secret of how to succeed. And yet I am dismissing it in a couple of pages. Many of the current crop of books on this subject concentrate on how to build your image through social media. Set up your own webpage. Do everything you can to be friends with people even more popular than yourself. Understand that you can use everything you do on the internet to develop your brand. What you post, what you like, what you've been doing, which causes you support can all be used to construct and project your brand.

No doubt this is true. But I prefer Jeff Bezos line of thinking:

> *A brand for a company is like a reputation for*
> *a person. You earn reputation by trying to do*
> *hard things well.*

If the image you project is the real you, there's nothing wrong with it. My problem with it is that it allows, and probably encourages, people to massage the truth if not brazenly lie. After all, most people, when given the opportunity, will present the best possible version of themselves. Many will edit the truth, Photoshop the pictures, and omit all that is negative. Why is it that almost everyone's life on Facebook is, paradoxically, so much better than almost everybody's real life (including their own)?

Which leads me on to what I believe is a really valuable piece of advice. Be honest, not just with yourself about yourself, but about yourself with other people. It's been my experience, working in various parts of the world and with people of many nationalities, that being honest, being true to yourself, really is the best policy.

13.1 COMMON LINGUISTIC ERRORS

A greater part of the world's troubles are due to questions of grammar.
Michel de Montaigne

Although we live in an inclusive, liberal, non-judgemental world, people are making judgements about others all the time.

Here are a few tips intended to save you from the more common linguistic solecisms. Sadly, any of these can mark you down immediately as poorly educated.

Issue	Explanation
adjectives for adverbs	Adjectives tell you about nouns; adverbs tell you about verbs. Both the following sentences are incorrect. "She ran the marathon really quick." It tells you how she ran, so it should be "quickly," not "quick." "He did really bad in his exams." It tells you how he did, so it should be "badly," not "bad."
emigrate immigrate	You "emigrate from"; you "immigrate to" a country.
exact extract	The dentist decided to exact revenge by extracting the tooth without any anaesthetic.
h (the letter)	The letter "h" is pronounced "aitch," **not** "haitch." Although the letter "h" at the start of a word generally represents an aspirate, the letter itself is spelled and pronounced "aitch."

I and me	**Use of "me" when it should be "I"**
	Someone asks "Who went into town?" You answer "Johnny and me [went into town]." Wrong! Strictly speaking, the answer should be "Johnny and I" because Johnny and I are the subject of the verb. You wouldn't say "Me went into town," so you shouldn't say "Johnny and me went into town."
	Use of "I" when it should be "me"
	The most common example of this error is when the personal pronouns are governed by a preposition. "He spent most of his time arguing with my wife and I." Wrong! "He spent most of his time arguing with my wife and me." You wouldn't say "He spent most of his time arguing with I."
	"Between you and I, he's naturally very argumentative." Wrong! It should be "Between you and me." Between is a preposition which takes an objective pronoun.
	The incorrect use of "me" when it should be "I" generally indicates simply ignorance of grammar.
	The incorrect use of "I" instead of "me" generally indicates a mistaken attempt to avoid a grammatical error, or a failed attempt to sound posher.

irregardless	"irregardless" is not a word. It's a confused fusion of the words "regardless" and "irrespective."
its and it's	**it's** is an abbreviation for **it is** or **it has**. "It's perfectly clear why 'it's' has an apostrophe – to indicate the missing letters." Some people think that "its" (i.e. "of it," a possessive pronoun) should also have an apostrophe to indicate the missing "of" – **but they're wrong**. "**It's** sad when a pub loses **its** licence." Rule: If "it's" is short for "it is" or "it has," it has an apostrophe; if it isn't, it doesn't.
literally	Use "literally" only where you mean that what you are saying actually happened. "He literally exploded with rage." Not very likely!
misunder-estimate	"misunderestimate" is not a word. It's a confused fusion of misunderstand and underestimate.
moot, mute	"moot" means debatable. I found it difficult to remain mute (silent, speechless) when the prime minister persisted in making moot points.
peak and pique	A disabled mountaineer who reaches the peak of a mountain may well pique (i.e. stimulate) your interest.
reign, rein	During his reign the king had free rein.

very	If something is "unique," it can't be "very unique." If something is excellent, it can't be "very excellent." Equally you can't be "a little bit pregnant." This is about using qualifying (usually intensifying) adverbs with absolute adjectives. Just use logic. If something is unique, it can't be more than unique. Something that is excellent can't be more than excellent. And you are either pregnant or you are not.
wet, whet	When something whets your appetite (i.e. sharpens it), your dry mouth may well become wet with saliva.
who, whom	"I wondered who was insulted." Correct. "I wondered who he was trying to insult." Wrong. It should be "I wondered whom he was trying to insult." Why? Because in the first example "who" stands for the subject of the verb "was insulted." The answer would be in the form "**I** was insulted," so it's "who," not "whom." In the second example "whom" is the object of the verb. The answer would be in the form "I was trying to insult **him**," so its "whom," not "who."

13.2 TRICKY PREPOSITIONS

This is the sort of English up with which I will not put.

(attributed to) Winston Churchill

according	"according to," "in accordance with"
acquaint	"acquaint" someone "with" something
acquiesce	"acquiesce in," not "acquiesce to"
aim	"aim at" a target; "aim to do" something
allude	"allude to" something, not "allude at"
analogous	"analogous to," rather than "analogous with"
angry	"angry with," rather than "angry at"
averse	"averse to" (although "from" might seem more logical)
annoyed	"annoyed with," rather than "at"
behalf	"on X's behalf," not "for X's behalf"
bored	"bored with" or "bored by," not "bored of"
borrow	"borrow from," not "borrow off"
compared	"compared to" when comparing unlike things "compared with" when comparing similar things
comprises	"comprises," not "comprises of"
conducive	"conducive to," not "conducive of"
different	"different from," not "to" or "than"
distribute	"distribute among," not "between"
equal	"equal to" not "equal as" or "equal with"
indifferent	"indifferent to"
inferior	"inferior to," not "inferior than"
in respect of	"in respect of," not "in respect to"

mean	"mean," not "mean for" ("I didn't mean this to happen")
oblivious	"oblivious to" (or, more rarely, "oblivious of")
part	"for X's part," rather than "on X's part"
prefer	"prefer a to b," not "prefer a than b"
protest	"protest against," rather than "protest at"
proud	"proud of," not "proud about"
similar	"similar to," not "similar as"
superior	"superior to," not "superior than"
tolerant	"tolerant of," not "tolerant to"

Yes, I know, we all make the odd mistake. And many would declare that, officially, the type of mistakes listed above are no longer of any consequence. But if you are concerned with managing your personal brand, surely it's best not to emit signals that could possibly damage it.

14
PERSONAL INTEGRITY

Who steals my purse steals trash; 'tis something, nothing;
'Twas mine, 'tis his, and has been slave to thousands;
But he that filches from me my good name
Robs me of that which not enriches him,
And makes me poor indeed.

Othello, William Shakespeare

Expanding on my thoughts about personal brand management, I want to emphasise the importance of personal integrity. I have found that if you are straight with people, most people will be straight with you. It's not always true, but I would say that most of the time it is. And when it is true, it can lay the foundations for an enduring and mutually beneficial relationship. Here's the mantra:

Always do what you say you will do – and do it
when you say you will do it.

14.1 BEING TRUE TO YOURSELF

This above all: to thine own self be true,
And it must follow, as the night the day,
Thou canst not then be false to any man.
Hamlet, William Shakespeare

It may seem odd that **being honest and true to yourself** should feature so prominently in a book about how to succeed. After all, there are so many stories in the media describing how many of the wealthiest people have made their fortunes by sharp practice, by dishonesty, by fraud or by avoiding tax. From politicians to bankers, from accountants to top businesspeople, stories of financial misdemeanours and other forms of chicanery abound.

There are two points I'd make. First, not all politicians, bankers, accountants, and business people are dishonest; it's just that the honest ones rarely feature in media headlines. Secondly, success is not just about making money. Very early in this book we considered the individual who wins the lottery. He or she is lucky, but not successful – or if successful, it's not because of winning the lottery.

Success is achieving your goal through your own ability and effort. We've listed what you need to do to succeed. You need to be focused, determined, and hardworking. And, I suggest, **you need to be honest with and about yourself.**

I realise that this recommendation goes against much received wisdom and, indeed, is contrary to the premise behind many self-help books. These sources of advice urge you to acquire new attributes, to assume new attitudes, to project an image that, by implication, is not what you are but what you aspire to be – a new you who will benefit from these enhancements if you can carry it off.

This is not my experience. There is no magic formula for success. There is certainly no one personality template. People with widely varied personalities can be successful. There are successful introverts and extroverts; successful leaders and successful powers behind the throne; successful team players and successful lone wolves. Far more important than any particular model of success is that you are true to yourself. Yes, major on your strengths; mitigate your weaknesses. **But be what you are; just be really good at it**. Your authenticity will trump any recently acquired and assumed attribute or attitude, however seemingly favourable.

14.2 BEING STRAIGHT WITH OTHERS

Integrity is doing the right thing, even when no one is watching.

C. S. Lewis

And while I'm in contrarian mode, I'd like to emphasis another aspect of personal integrity: namely, being honest and straight with others. I'm not sure this suggestion is advice. It runs counter to the zeitgeist of the times where almost every supplier of goods and services is using every trick in the book to separate you from your money. (The billions of dollars and billions of pounds our global financial institutions have been fined for mis-selling, money laundering, and rate fixing are merely the most obvious and egregious examples of endemic institutional dishonesty.) But my advocacy of honesty is a serious suggestion that comes from my personal experience in business.

Always do what you say you will do – and do it when you say you will do it. I found this was a good principle in the UK where my company provided media coverage analysis services for most UK government departments and many banks and other leading commercial institutions. And I also found it to be true in our work overseas.

For many years, I worked the market in Saudi Arabia, providing media consultancy services to the Saudi Ministry of Information. On my numerous visits to the Kingdom I would meet other Brits doing business there. "Getting paid is a real problem," I was told. "They're very slow payers. They will pick you up on the slightest glitch and use that as an excuse not to pay you."

Not surprisingly I was wary. I studied very carefully every clause in the contracts I was asked to sign, and made sure I was confident we could fulfil our responsibilities and meet all the deadlines. And that's what we did – always precisely and always on time. And in thirty years of doing business in Saudi Arabia I was never not paid. Occasionally there were delays because of administrative problems, but in the end every riyal for which I invoiced was handed over to my company.

I went back to the complaining Brits and probed a little. "Yes, we were a bit late in completing the project, but we had a problem with our supplier," said one. "When it came to it, we had to use another material, but it was just as good as the one specified," said another. By now I knew how the system worked. Government contracts were policed by an army of Egyptian or Syrian lawyers. It was their job to make sure their employers got what they paid for. They went through contracts with a fine-tooth comb. After all, that's what they were paid to do. If you hadn't met the terms of the contract, you were in trouble. Delays of payment or worse could ensue. But if you did what you said you would do and did it when you said you would do it, you were home free.

Whether you're signing multi-million pound contracts, organising a project, or just arranging to meet friends, **do what you say you will do – and do it when you say you will do it**.

It's a pretty good principle. In the long run and in the real world, it will do more for your brand than a thousand finely tuned tweets and any number of Photoshopped pictures on Facebook.

14.3 TAKING RESPONSIBILITY

> *The price of greatness is responsibility.*
> Winston Churchill

In this book, I argue that you should take control of your life, that you should always keep in mind that you can change course, that you can always take a **Decision**. If you accept that you can do this, you have power.

Back in the day, many people stayed in the same job, or at least worked for the same company, all their lives. Even when they reached the middle years of their working life and they were bored and disillusioned, they stayed. They served their time, waiting for the longed-for retirement. They made a choice, but not a **Decision**. They did what seemed obvious, sensible, safe. But they lost control of their working lives.

If you are unfulfilled in your job and unhappy with your prospects, you can move to another company. If you are unhappy with the type of work you are doing, you can change careers. Of course, there are challenges and risks. But you should know that you can rise to the challenge.

And when you have assessed the risk, be driven by reason rather than fear. Fear eats the soul.[4] Then, and only then, can you make an informed choice and, hopefully, take the right **Decision**.

But with power comes responsibility. If, after squaring up to the challenge and assessing the risk, you decide to proceed, you have to take responsibility for your **Decision**.

I won't, although I'm tempted, to give responsibility a capital R (just as I gave Decision a capital D) because again I mean rather more than is normally meant by the word. Everyone has to accept some responsibility for their choices. There is no alternative; you have to take the consequences. But here I'm using "taking responsibility" to mean something more. I mean welcoming responsibility because it is the direct consequence of your **Decision**. You have taken control of your life. Whatever the consequences, they are yours, so own them.

When I set up Panarc International Ltd, I knew the company might fail. I had no capital and a strong aversion to borrowing. I was not keen on, or adept at, networking. And I knew most new companies failed. I was in my late thirties – in business terms, "in my prime." I had at least fifteen years of high earning and top-class benefits as an employee in prospect. But I still went ahead.

Why?

There were two reasons, of which the second was more important than the first. First, I had an idea for a business and I was convinced it was a good idea. Secondly, and most importantly, I knew that if I didn't give it a try, at the end of my life I would regret it.

---

[4] *Fear Eats the Soul* is the title of a Rainer Werner Fassbinder film – a great title and a great film.

Was it a risk?

Yes, of course it was a risk. And today I am well aware that we live in an extraordinarily risk-averse society so I fully understand many people's reluctance to take a chance. But the willingness to take a risk is an essential component of success.

Don't misunderstand me. I don't mean that I approve of gambling. And I don't mean that you should take risks without thinking things through, without considering the different possible outcomes and the likelihood of success. But I do believe that there come times in life when you need to take a **Decision** about something, and almost always there is risk involved. And when faced with an element of risk, too often fear outweighs everything else. Learn to sneer at fear.

If, after careful consideration of all the factors and despite the risk, you decide to go ahead, you will feel a sense of empowerment. You have taken charge of your life and responsibility for it. And you will deserve to succeed.

14.4 ADMITTING MISTAKES

A good leader takes a little more than his share of
the blame, a little less than his share of the credit.

Arnold H. Glasow

And that means that you personally have to take responsibility for bad decisions as well as good; for failure as well as success. This is a good principle in business and in life. When something goes wrong, the first reaction of many people is to shift the blame, to find an excuse, to make light of or trivialise the damage. It's a natural human reaction – but it's unhealthy.

Trying to put the blame on others (even if they are partly to blame) is generally pointless and counterproductive. It diminishes you in the eyes of others and antagonises whomever you are sharing the blame with. (If they are partly to blame, they and others will know it and respect you for shouldering more than your fair share of responsibility.) Making excuses again indicates weakness. If anyone asks you to explain, give an objective reason for the failure. (There is a difference between a reason and an excuse.) And as for trivialising any harm, making light of the damage is unrealistic and again smacks of weakness or stupidity.

When I first worked for the Swiss pharmaceutical company, I became accustomed to attending management meetings as the Market Research Manager. As commonly happens, despite the best efforts of the MD and a written agenda, the meetings tended to degenerate into discursive and inconclusive discussions of a wide range of issues, many of which were way off point. The MD seemed to think everyone should have their say.

After three years, I moved into marketing and, at the same time, a new MD was appointed. He introduced two innovations for meetings that seemed to me very sensible and very effective. First, he announced that in future no one would be allowed to mention at the meeting anyone who wasn't present. Secondly, any discussion at the meeting was to end with one or more action points, allocated to someone present and noted alongside the relevant minute.

The first convention prevented any committee member from blaming one of his subordinates for a failure. If a deadline had been missed the manager whose department had failed was held personally and directly accountable. Managers had the authority and power to run their departments, so they had direct responsibility for its success or failure.

The second convention ensured that only items where action was required appeared on the agenda, and that where action was determined, someone was charged with implementing it. At the next meeting, woe betide anyone who had failed to deal with an action point allocated to them.

I approved of these measures. They forced managers to take personal responsibility for whatever happened in the domain. Management meetings became more focused and shorter. And it taught me to take personal responsibility for failures as well as success.

And there's something else. As noted elsewhere, mistakes provide an opportunity to learn some incredibly valuable life lessons. In my case, success has, on some occasions, led to overconfidence, arrogance, and complacency. Failure has forced me to understand where and why I went wrong, engendered a healthy dose of humility, and motivated me to try harder. So you can see which of the two (success or failure) is more instructive.

When I left school to go up to New College, Oxford, I worked hard in the first two terms. At the end, I took the Prelims exams. When the results were published, I was not a little surprised. I had been awarded a distinction. Out of the hundreds of students in the English faculty that year, only five distinctions were awarded – and I was one of them. The other four were girls. So out of the hundreds of male Oxford undergraduates reading English that year, I was the only one to be awarded a distinction.

Sadly, what seemed a triumph and recognition of my extraordinary abilities, turned out to be a disaster. To begin with I couldn't believe it. Then the hubris began. I had been worried about making the grade at New College, but with a modest amount of work, I had achieved my highest academic award to date in the intensely competitive world of Oxford academia.

I was fit, I was young, and obviously I was brilliant. Arrogance and complacency followed.

My second year at New College was really enjoyable. I had about ten close friends, all but one of them grammar school boys. It is often said that state school boys fear that they will be looked down upon by the generally better-educated and certainly better-off students from public school. I can honestly say that I never experienced any prejudice at Oxford, despite the fact that I was from a state school and still had, as I have to this day, a London accent. (Actually that's not strictly true. There was arrogance, but it came from us, the grammar school boys. We had competed against the entire population to win a place at Oxford. Many from public schools had gained entrance on closed scholarships.)

In that second year, we talked a lot, we drank a lot, and some of us spent any free time chasing girls. On the study front, I ignored all lectures (in five years at Oxford, I attended only one lecture). I did attend all my tutorials and did whatever work was required of me, but no more. Most of my time I spent enjoying myself. When the weather was good, I punted on the Cherwell – and became an expert, capable of sending my punt scudding through the water at remarkably high speeds and effecting amazingly precise, high-speed manoeuvres through dexterous use of the punting pole.

At the end of the third year, I took Finals (the final set of exams for the BA Honours degree). I had covered the syllabus in the last year, putting in sufficient effort, or so I thought, to get a satisfactory result. After all, with roughly the same amount of effort, I had earned one of five distinctions in Prelims, and although First-Class Honours degrees were in strictly limited supply at that time, there were certainly more than five awarded each year in the English faculty. I sat the exams. All went well as far as I could tell. It seems unbelievable but I was entirely unconcerned that I had failed to attend any of the lectures given by the Fellows who would be setting and marking the exam papers.

There are, or were then, four classes of degree at Oxford – First, Second, Third, and Fourth, plus an aegrotat if you were too ill to take the exams. The results were published. I had been given a Second-Class Honours degree. I was bitterly disappointed. I was surprised. And I was determined that this would not be the end of my academic career. I am not academic but I am competitive, and I was deeply disappointed by a Second-Class degree.

Had I been given a First, I would have left Oxford to seek my fortune in London. As it was, I was determined not to leave until I had restored my self-esteem. I looked for a higher degree involving examinations. The only one on offer was the oddly-named B.Phil. (later renamed M.Phil.). The B.Phil in Modern English Studies had only just been established as a degree and was Oxford's first higher degree that involved exams. To acquire a B.Phil, you had to commit to a two-year course, at the end of which you had to take five three-hour examination papers and submit a 20,000 word thesis. This was just what I wanted.

I applied through my New College tutor to be registered for the B.Phil and was accepted. My enthusiasm was increased, rather than diminished, when halfway through my course, the results for the first year of the B.Phil in Modern English Studies were published. There was only Pass or Fail. All the candidates had failed. Clearly the university was determined to show they were setting a very high bar for this new degree. I worked really hard throughout the two years of the course and especially hard in the second year.

At the end of two years' postgraduate study, I submitted my thesis; I took the exams. And waited. There were three of us at New College who took the B.Phil that year – me and two Americans. I passed. One American passed. The other failed and left Oxford, I guess, with nothing other than memories of two years spent among the dreaming spires.

For me, honour was satisfied. I had passed exams that those with First-Class Honours degrees had failed. Now I could leave Oxford.

Looking back, I regret not working hard enough as an undergraduate. Sadly, the distinction I was awarded in Prelims engendered in me a highly enjoyable but entirely spurious sense of intellectual invincibility.

But at least I learned the crucial lesson: **If I wanted to succeed at anything, I had to work hard.** I had identified a character weakness in myself that, on reflection, had been evident throughout my school years. If I succeeded at something, I tended to become complacent, or worse, arrogant. And then, inevitably, my performance deteriorated and I disappointed myself. I determined I must never let that happen again.

I also acknowledged another general lesson: **If you really want something, never give up** (see 2.2 Determination).

14.5 BEING FAIR

Before you take sides, hear both sides.
Anon

In every organisation the plan is that everything should run smoothly. There are systems that have been tested and refined. There are trained staff to follow procedures. There are managers to ensure best practice is followed. There are clear communication channels to ensure everyone is kept informed. At least, that's the plan.

But sometimes things go wrong.

Well, as they say, success has many fathers; failure is an orphan.

What should you do in such circumstances?

First, analyse the situation and determine the cause of the problem. In a business there are often several causes. For example:

- An instruction wasn't clearly expressed.
- Even if it was clearly expressed, it wasn't fully understood.
- No one checked to see whether the instruction had been followed.
- There was a delay because the department responsible for following the instruction had other priorities.
- The part you ordered was out of stock.
- It was sent but delivered to the wrong address.
- It arrived but it was too late or defective.

Secondly, make sure you know exactly what happened. Do this as objectively as you can. Why? So that you can see where the weakness is and make sure it doesn't happen again.

And because, in the inevitable autopsy, you need to be able to speak with honesty and authority. While others involved are likely to be keen to shift the blame, you will be the calm voice of good sense. You are the constructive one who knows exactly why it happened and how to prevent it in future – and you can fairly identify who is truly responsible.

14.6 FEWER RULES; MORE EXAMPLES

> *An ounce of practice is worth more than tons of preaching.*
>
> Mahatma Gandhi

I saw this invaluable advice (fewer rules; more examples) painted in massive letters on a tall brick wall in Southampton. It is, I believe, relevant in parenting, business, management, and life. A bold claim, yes! But I stand by it.

The world is full of rules. They are used by people in power to impose their will on those without. Of course, it is true that civilisation depends upon the rule of law. And it is true that we all need standards that we aspire to meet, by which we can judge ourselves and others. But what is the best way of promoting these standards?

If a parent wishes to persuade a child not to steal, which is the better way, to order the child not to steal or always to be honest?

It's easier and quicker to order the child, but teaching him/her to always be honest by example will be more persuasive. Certainly, if you order the child not to steal and then steal yourself, you really can't expect the child to obey your command, much less respect you in other matters.

My wife and I were blessed with a son and a daughter. Neither of us felt the urge or the need to impose sets of rules on our kids. But we did explain to them that:

- actions had consequences (this was not a rule but a fact)
- others had the same rights as them (not a provable fact but not a rule; simply an essential precept for a civilised society)
- they should always aspire to be the best they could be at whatever they chose to do (advice for their own satisfaction)

We didn't force them to work hard at school, but we did explain to them that if they didn't, it was unlikely they would get a good job, enjoy a comfortable life, or feel personally fulfilled.

If one of them took the other's favourite toy, we didn't take it from them; we gave the offender's favourite toy to the victim.

And, as for working hard, they saw what their parents did.

When I set up Panarc International, like most people who set up a business, I led by example. I started earlier than everyone else; I finished later. And in the early years, I took less money than most of those I employed, and much less than I had earned as an employee. It was my decision to form a company; it was my responsibility to make it work. Not being the most empathic of people, I cannot say exactly how my staff felt, but this much is true:

- They all worked hard.
- Many of them stayed with me for many years.

Did this philosophy work in bringing up our children? I can't say. We may well have simply been lucky. But both our kids have grown up to be responsible, independently minded, conscientious, and extremely industrious adults – and successful. So I guess, at the least, our approach to parenting didn't do them any harm.

So I say again: **Fewer rules; more examples**.

15
RISK

There is a tide in the affairs of men,
Which, taken at the flood, leads on to fortune;
Omitted, all the voyage of their life
Is bound in shallows and in miseries.

Julius Caesar, William Shakespeare

Risk has negative connotations. Risk is defined as "full of the possibility of danger, failure and loss." We are advised to avoid unnecessary risks. (Rarely are we urged to take necessary risks, although if they are necessary, we would, presumably, be well advised to take them.)

This advice to be cautious is generally prudent and wise. Taking a risk means, to some extent, heading into the unknown. The known is safe. We feel secure in the known. Even if the existing situation is unsatisfactory, we know what to expect. The unknown, on the other hand, could be worse than unsatisfactory; it could be disastrous. So we should be wary of risk. After all, I was pretty scathing about financial advisers who gamble with our savings and I warned against traders on the stock market who feel free to take serious risks with other people's money.

So we can agree that, in general, risks, especially unnecessary ones, are to be avoided.

But that said, almost all progress depends on someone taking a risk. Someone had to take a chance on first eating all the fruit and vegetables that form a staple part of our diet today. The first man to nibble rhubarb leaves had a bad stomach, but he or one of his friends persisted and found the stalks nutritious. Someone decided to steam cashew nuts and eat them despite the fact that when his friend had eaten them raw, he had fallen ill. And as for mushrooms – well, the pioneers were dicing with death, as is anyone, other than a mycologist, who eats random fungi today.

Edward Jenner took a risk in 1796 when he inoculated the eight-year-old James Phipps with a vaccine derived from cowpox. He could have killed the boy and destroyed his reputation as a respected physician. Instead, he saved millions of lives and assured his place in the pantheon of eminent physicians. Steve Jobs took risks with his Macintosh computer. Elon Musk faced seemingly insuperable odds and probable bankruptcy with the Tesla car and SpaceX. Sylvester Stallone took a risk with *Rocky* when he refused all offers for the script until someone agreed to let him play the lead role.

It's obvious that risk is an essential requirement if people are to move forward, to acquire new knowledge, to expand their horizons, to fulfil their potential. It was true for them and the same is true for you. At some point, or points, in your life, if you want to progress, you will have to take a risk.

And there's something else. **You can't avoid risk. Deciding to do nothing involves risk. You risk all the lost opportunities of doing something. Deciding not to take any chances involves a risk. You miss all the benefits those chances might have offered.**

So how do you know when to err on the side of caution and when to take a leap in the dark? That's one of the most difficult questions we ever face.

Obviously you should attempt to assess the degree of risk involved, the possible rewards of success and the cost of failure. Sadly, such an assessment is likely to be largely guesswork. The risk you are thinking of taking is almost certainly one you haven't taken before. It may be one that no one has taken before. So how can you know the answers? Sorry, but that's part of the challenge – and that's why it's a risk.

But there are some key questions you can ask and answer with some certainty:

- Do you really believe in the project?
- Are you prepared to give the project everything you've got?
- Can you face the possibility of failure?
- Will you always regret it if you don't try?

If your answer to these four questions is an unequivocal "Yes," then go ahead. You will almost certainly succeed.

My only caveat is this: if, in the inevitably darker moments on your path to success, you realise you're in a tunnel, not a cave, cut your losses. Come out into the daylight and wait for another better chance to take a risk.

And when it comes, if your answer to the four key questions above is "Yes," and you follow the advice in this book, your success is assured.

16
SUMMARY OF ADVICE

1. At some point in your life, you will have to take a **Decision**. Such decisions are counterintuitive, bloody-minded, against the flow and inherently risky. Perhaps it's not surprising that many people tend to shy away from them.

2. Most of our lives we have the opportunity to make life-changing **Decisions**. It's our fault if we choose not to make them.

3. Always focus on your goal and choose a path that at least offers the possibility of success.

4. In response to any challenge, say to yourself, "**Yes**, we can do this **if** … ." Banish from your mind any response that begins, "**No**, we can't do this **because** … ."

5. Turn every mistake into a lesson.

6. If you can't fix it, park it.

7. Multitasking is simply an excuse for failing to do anything really well.

8. Get your head down, put your fingers in your ears, and concentrate.

9. Determination is not the key to success, but it is a prerequisite.

10. The difference between success and failure is often much less than we imagine; just one more punch, just one more try.

11. You never know when you are going to win. You just have to keep trying until you find out.

12. Those with less talent can succeed with hard work; those with more talent will fail without it.

13. Success is 10% inspiration, 20% concentration, 30% determination and 40% hard work.

14. Nowhere have I said that being very bright, intellectually accomplished, in possession of an outstanding IQ, is a requirement for success. Because it isn't.

15. The concept of work/life balance is a rhetorical trick to strengthen the argument that work should be downgraded in importance to allow "life" to flourish.

16. Acquire the habit of self-criticism to ensure that you are being and doing the best you can.

17. You need to précis tasks just as you précis articles. If there isn't time to perform the whole task to 99% perfection, then précis the task and perform the key elements of the whole task to the highest level you can in the time available.

18. To be "lucky," you just need to be open to possibilities and opportunities.

19. All my advice depends on acceptance of the primacy of reason.

20. When writing, there are three basic principles that should guide you: clarity, simplicity, and brevity.

21. Think before you write. A written record of what you say and to whom you say it can turn out to be your best friend or your worst enemy.

22. You should see numbers as your friends. Numbers are honest and reliable, not like words, which can be ambiguous at least and, in the mouth of a liar, misleading and deceitful.

23. While empathy is a core skill of the greatest importance it can also be the most difficult for a highly focused and determined individual to exercise.

24. Whether you are motivating or disciplining staff, or negotiating a deal, or simply arguing a case, think of how you would feel if you were the other party.

25. I'm a strong believer in lists – in particular, in lists of things to do.

26. Always remember, your priorities are not necessarily the same as those of other people.

27. Learn to listen. And listen to learn.

28. Timing, like the weather, is difficult to get right.

29. Perception is deceptive. Reality rules, OK.

30. There is a real world. There is good and bad; there is winning and losing; there is success and failure. In the end, reality asserts itself.

31. Never mistake a cave for a tunnel.

32. When negotiating, you should use your strengths judiciously, reserving them for the attainment of your core objectives.

33. Politics in business is a complex world in which reason and emotion rub shoulders, in which personal ambition often takes precedence over the interests of the company, in which personal likes and dislikes, prejudices, and preconceptions play a part in important decisions.

34. As you progress up the management ladder, you will find that success depends less and less on competence and more and more on political acumen and general clubbability.

35. "The customer is always right," and "The biggest problem with running any business is the customers." You'll hear both sentiments widely expressed. And both are true.

36. If you are providing a service to a client, the best foundation for a lasting relationship is to replicate all the attributes of a friendship.

37. Simply looking for ways to make things better creates an opportunity to be creative.

38. Analogical thinking generates metaphors and similes. It enables us to see parallels between unconnected spheres of thought and can be used as a means of generating creative ideas.

39. If you keep a lookout for opportunities, they will find you.

40. There are good accountants, architects, doctors, engineers, financial advisers, surgeons, and surveyors, and there are bad ones.

41. The only way the financial services sector can make money is by making money out of your money.

42. In any relationship where two people have an interest in the same sum of money, each of the parties will give precedence to their own interests.

43. Beware when you let other people gamble with your money.

44. Never borrow unless you have to.

45. Save, not to earn the currently derisory levels of interest but simply to assert your freedom from the shackles of debt.

46. Property is probably the best of all long-term investments.

47. It's been my experience, working in various parts of the world and with people of many nationalities, that being honest, being true to yourself, really is the best policy.

48. Be what you are. Your authenticity will trump any recently acquired and assumed attribute or attitude, however seemingly favourable.

49. Whether you're signing multimillion-pound contracts, organising a project or just arranging to meet friends, do what you say you will do – and do it when you say you will do it.

50. Fewer rules; more examples.

51. Deciding to do nothing involves risk. You risk all the lost opportunities of doing something. Deciding not to take any chances involves a risk. You miss all the benefits those chances might have offered.

52. Acknowledge and mitigate your weaknesses; exercise, enhance, and play to your strengths; always seek to do better; never lose faith; and be true to yourself.

CONCLUSION

It's been quite a journey.

After careful introspection, you have identified your goal in life and have set out on the path to reach it. And I have given you the best advice I can to help you to succeed.

You are left to do the heavy lifting, but I have at least been clear about what you need to do. I have identified some of the dangers you will face and suggested how to avoid or deal with them. And I have given pointers on how to discern and exploit opportunities.

I believe if you put into practice just half the advice I have given, you will be successful.

And I have been honest about what is required of you. You will have to work hard. For some, this will be a disappointment, but if you're honest, you knew this would be so. Anyone who tells you otherwise is either stupid or a snake-oil salesman, or both.

Some of my advice conforms to the conventional wisdom of business advisers; the rest may strike you as counterintuitive or even eccentric, but all of it represents conclusions drawn from my own experience over many years in various industries. The media coverage analysis service (which Panarc International pioneered and which we maintained successfully for almost three decades) brought us, as clients, many UK government departments, a number of overseas governments and a very wide range of non-governmental and commercial organisations, including the BBC, BT, many banks, and a number of charities. It gave me the opportunity to observe and assess the different strategies and tactics that we all employ in order to achieve our goals. From my own experience and my observations of others, I was able to distil what works best and what is counterproductive.

Of course, I'm not suggesting that my way is the only way to achieve your goals. There are many examples of men and women who have acquired fame and great wealth without following my advice. Some have employed dubious or dishonest means; others have simply used others' efforts and abilities to enrich themselves; some have bullied, beaten or conned their way to the top; and others have just been lucky. But such people do not meet the criteria for success set out in this book – achieving your goals fairly through your own talents and efforts – nor can they guarantee success to those who follow their example.

Every one of us has strengths and weaknesses. I'm quick, focused and hardworking, but I'm not a spontaneously empathic person. I'm pretty sure I wouldn't score highly on the scale of emotional intelligence (although I try), and while fully recognising its value, I find networking so tedious that I have rarely, if ever, engaged in it. You too will have you own combinations of strengths and weaknesses and I would not for a moment pretend that every bit of my advice is equally pertinent to every reader. But I do believe that the principles I have identified and defined will work for everyone.

If I had to encapsulate my advice in a few words it would be this.

Always seek to do better;
be true to yourself;
open your mind;
keep positive;
sneer at fear;
never give up.

If you adopt this philosophy as your guiding principle and follow, in general, the practical advice in this book, you cannot fail to succeed.

APPENDICES

Appendix A │ List of poems

Learn some of these poems off by heart and you will have internalised some of the best poems in the English language. Learning any of them will exercise your mind and improve your powers of concentration. Internalising them will make you a richer and more interesting person.

Matthew Arnold, "Dover Beach"

William Blake, "A Poison Tree"

William Blake, "The Sick Rose"

William Blake, "The Tyger"

Walter de la Mare, "The Listeners"

John Donne, "Death, be not proud"

John Donne, "Song" ("Go and catch a falling star")

Robert Frost, "The Road Not Taken"

Thomas Hardy, "In Time of 'The Breaking of Nations'"

George Herbert, "Love"

Gerard Manley Hopkins, "Pied Beauty"

Gerard Manley Hopkins, "The Windhover"

Gerard Manley Hopkins, "Thou art indeed just, Lord, if I contend"

John Keats, "On First Looking into Chapman's Homer"

John Keats, "A thing of beauty is a joy for ever" (from *Endymion*)

John Keats, "Bright star, would I were stedfast as thou art"

Rudyard Kipling, "If – "

Richard Lovelace, "Stone walls do not a prison make" (from "To Althea, from Prison")

Richard Lovelace, "The Scrutiny"

John Masefield, "Cargoes"

John Milton, "On His Blindness"

Christina Rossetti, "Remember"

William Shakespeare, "Let me not to the marriage of true minds" (Sonnet 116)

William Shakespeare, "Shall I compare thee to a summer's day?" (Sonnet 18)

William Shakespeare, "Th'expense of spirit in a waste of shame" (Sonnet 129)

Percy Bysshe Shelley, "Ozymandias"

Sir John Suckling, "Song" (Out upon it, I have lov'd)

Alfred, Lord Tennyson, "Frater Ave Atque Vale"

Dylan Thomas, "Do not go gentle into that good night"

William Wordsworth, "Composed upon Westminster Bridge"

William Wordsworth, "The world is too much with us; late and soon"

William Butler Yeats, "Father and Child"

William Butler Yeats, "Long-Legged Fly"

Appendix B | Grouping

When grouping a set of data, we should perhaps emphasise the adding of meaning. In any set of data, there is, of course, meaning in each of the units that make up the set, but grouping allows you to add meaning simply by the act of grouping. Grouping tells the reader the criterion the grouper is applying in order to construct the group. That criterion is itself an additional unit of meaning.

Here's a very simple example. Take a set of eight people:

a tall clever man	a tall clever woman
a short clever man	a tall stupid man
a short stupid man	a short clever woman
a tall stupid woman	a short stupid woman

If I group this set:

Group 1: tall clever man; tall stupid man, tall clever woman; tall stupid woman

Group 2: short clever man; short stupid man; short clever woman; short stupid woman

I am directing your attention to the height of the people in the group.

If I group the set:

Group 1: a tall clever man; a short clever man; a tall stupid man; a short stupid man

Group 2: a tall clever woman; a short clever woman; a tall stupid woman; a short stupid woman

I am directing your attention to the gender of the people in the group.

If I group the set:

Group 1: a tall clever man; a short clever man; a tall clever woman; a short clever woman

Group 2: a tall stupid man; a short stupid man; a tall stupid woman; a short stupid woman

I am directing your attention to the intellectual capacity of the people in the group.

Grouping allows us to organise a set of data into meaningful clusters.

Below I give an example of grouping a set of arguments in various ways. In each case, we add order and meaning to the set of data simply by the act of grouping.

I've chosen the issue of capital punishment to show that even a subject that generates high and often irrational sentiment can be subjected to a systematic analysis based on various criteria.

Grouping a set of arguments

Let's look at the issue of capital punishment and list some of the arguments presented in any debate of the subject. Below we set out a set of arguments.

1. Capital punishment, after due legal process, is a legitimate punishment.

2. Capital punishment degrades those who administer it.

3. Capital punishment denies the possibility of redemption.

4. Capital punishment gives closure to the relatives of the victim.

5. Capital punishment is a cruel and inhumane punishment.

6. Capital punishment is an effective deterrent.

7. Capital punishment is barbaric.

8. Capital punishment is cheaper for the state/taxpayer than keeping murderers in prison.

9. Capital punishment is justified on the "eye for an eye" principle.

10. Capital punishment is state murder.

11. Capital punishment is the only proportionate punishment for murder.

12. Capital punishment is too kind to the murderer.

13. Capital punishment precludes the possibility of repeat offending.

14. Capital punishment violates an individual's human rights.

15. Hundreds of innocent lives have been lost when released murderers reoffend.

16. Some murderers are so evil they defile the world and should be exterminated.

17. The murder rate increases in societies where capital punishment has been abolished.

18. The murder rate is unaffected by the abolition of capital punishment.

19. There are proven cases of the execution of innocent individuals.

20. There is always the risk that you execute an innocent person.

21. "Vengeance is mine," saith the Lord.

The list is not ordered, or rather it is in alphabetical order, which is meaningless in this case because it all depends on how each sentence has been formulated. (We could move number 21 to the top slot simply by expressing it thus: "As the bible says, 'Vengeance is mine,' saith the Lord.")

So how can we bring order out of chaos? There are many ways, but first we must decide on our aim.

If we wish to analyse the issue as a whole, we would probably begin by dividing the list into arguments for and arguments against:

Arguments for capital punishment

1. Capital punishment, after due legal process, is a legitimate punishment.
2. Capital punishment gives closure to the relatives of the victim.
3. Capital punishment is an effective deterrent.
4. Capital punishment is cheaper for the state/taxpayer than keeping murderers in prison.
5. Capital punishment is justified on the "eye for an eye" principle.
6. Capital punishment is the only proportionate punishment for murder.
7. Capital punishment precludes the possibility of repeat offending.
8. Hundreds of innocent lives have been lost when released murderers reoffend.
9. Some murderers are so evil they defile the world and should be exterminated.
10. The murder rate increases in societies where capital punishment has been abolished.

Arguments against capital punishment

1. Capital punishment degrades those who administer it.
2. Capital punishment denies the possibility of redemption.
3. Capital punishment is a cruel and inhumane punishment.
4. Capital punishment is barbaric.

5. Capital punishment is state murder.

6. Capital punishment is too kind to the murderer.

7. Capital punishment violates an individual's human rights.

8. The murder rate is unaffected by the abolition of capital punishment.

9. There are proven cases of the execution of innocent individuals.

10. There is always the risk that you execute an innocent person.

11. "Vengeance is mine," saith the Lord

On the other hand, we might wish to distinguish between those **arguments based on evidence** and those based on other **non-evidential drivers** (e.g. emotion, religion):

Evidence-based arguments

1. Capital punishment degrades those who administer it.

2. Capital punishment gives closure to the relatives of the victim.

3. Capital punishment is an effective deterrent.

4. Capital punishment is cheaper for the state/taxpayer than keeping murderers in prison.

5. Hundreds of innocent lives have been lost when released murderers reoffend.

6. The murder rate increases in societies where capital punishment has been abolished.

7. The murder rate is unaffected by the abolition of capital punishment.

8. There are proven cases of the execution of innocent individuals.

9. There is always the risk that you execute an innocent person.

We are assuming that it would be possible to gather evidence on whether those who administer capital punishment are degraded and that we could find evidence of the extent to which capital punishment gives the relatives of victims closure.

Non-evidence-based arguments

1. Capital punishment, after due legal process, is a legitimate punishment.
2. Capital punishment denies the possibility of redemption.
3. Capital punishment is a cruel and inhumane punishment.
4. Capital punishment is barbaric.
5. Capital punishment is justified on the "eye for an eye" principle.
6. Capital punishment is state murder.
7. Capital punishment is the only proportionate punishment for murder.
8. Capital punishment is too kind to the murderer.
9. Capital punishment violates an individual's human rights.
10. Capital punishment precludes the possibility of repeat offending.
11. Some murderers are so evil they defile the world and should be exterminated.
12. "Vengeance is mine," saith the Lord.

Or again, we might wish to distinguish between those arguments which are **incontrovertibly true** and those that are **open to debate**:

Arguments incontrovertibly true

1. Capital punishment, after due legal process, is a legitimate punishment.

2. Capital punishment denies the possibility of redemption.

3. Capital punishment is cheaper for the state/taxpayer than keeping murderers in prison.

4. Capital punishment violates an individual's human rights.

5. Capital punishment precludes the possibility of repeat offending.

6. Hundreds of innocent lives have been lost when released murderers reoffend.

7. There are proven cases of the execution of innocent individuals.

8. There is always the risk that you execute an innocent person.

Argument 1 is true in its own terms because it is circular. Capital punishment must be legitimate (i.e. legal) if it is endorsed by due legal process.

Argument 4 is true if we accept Amnesty International's interpretation of the UN's definition of human rights, which recognises each person's right to life and categorically states that "No one shall be subjected to torture or to cruel, inhuman or degrading treatment or punishment."

Arguments open to debate

1. Capital punishment degrades those who administer it.

2. Capital punishment gives closure to the relatives of the victim.

3. Capital punishment is a cruel and inhumane punishment.

4. Capital punishment is an effective deterrent.

5. Capital punishment is barbaric.

6. Capital punishment is justified on the "eye for an eye" principle.

7. Capital punishment is state murder.

8. Capital punishment is the only proportionate punishment for murder.

9. Capital punishment is too kind to the murderer.

10. Some murderers are so evil they defile the world and should be exterminated.

11. The murder rate increases in societies where capital punishment has been abolished.

12. The murder rate is unaffected by the abolition of capital punishment.

13. "Vengeance is mine," saith the Lord.

Or yet again, we might want to be more precise in our analysis of all the different drivers that lie behind the various arguments. Now we will find arguments falling in to more than one category:

Rational arguments

1. Capital punishment, after due legal process, is a legitimate punishment.

2. Capital punishment denies the possibility of redemption.

3. Capital punishment is an effective deterrent.

4. Capital punishment is cheaper for the state/taxpayer than keeping murderers in prison.

5. Capital punishment precludes the possibility of repeat offending.

6. Hundreds of innocent lives have been lost when released murderers reoffend.

7. There is always the risk that you execute an innocent person.

Arguments from authority

1. Capital punishment, after due legal process, is a legitimate punishment.

2. Capital punishment is a cruel and inhumane punishment.

3. Capital punishment is justified on the "eye for an eye" principle.

4. "Vengeance is mine," saith the Lord

Emotional arguments

1. Capital punishment degrades those who administer it.

2. Capital punishment gives closure to the relatives of the victim.

3. Capital punishment is a cruel and inhumane punishment.

4. Capital punishment is barbaric.

5. Capital punishment is state murder.

6. Capital punishment is the only proportionate punishment for murder.

7. Capital punishment is too kind to the murderer.

8. Some murderers are so evil they defile the world and should be exterminated.

Moral arguments

1. Capital punishment degrades those who administer it.

2. Capital punishment denies the possibility of redemption.

3. Capital punishment gives closure to the relatives of the victim.

4. Capital punishment is a cruel and inhumane punishment.

5. Capital punishment is barbaric.

6. Capital punishment is justified on the "eye for an eye" principle.

7. Capital punishment is state murder.

8. Capital punishment violates an individual's human rights.

9. The murder rate increases in societies where capital punishment has been abolished.

10. There are proven cases of the execution of innocent individuals.

11. There is always the risk that you execute an innocent person.

Practical/economic arguments

1. Capital punishment is an effective deterrent.

2. Capital punishment is cheaper for the state/taxpayer than keeping murderers in prison.

3. Capital punishment precludes the possibility of repeat offending.

4. Hundreds of innocent lives have been lost when released murderers reoffend.

5. The murder rate increases in societies where capital punishment has been abolished.

6. The murder rate is unaffected by the abolition of capital punishment.

Evidence-based arguments

1. Capital punishment degrades those who administer it.

2. Capital punishment gives closure to the relatives of the victim.

3. Capital punishment is an effective deterrent.

4. Capital punishment is cheaper for the state/taxpayer than keeping murderers in prison.

5. Hundreds of innocent lives have been lost when released murderers reoffend.

6. The murder rate increases in societies where capital punishment has been abolished.

7. The murder rate is unaffected by the abolition of capital punishment.

8. The murder rate increases in societies where capital punishment has been abolished.

9. There are proven cases of the execution of innocent individuals.

10. There is always the risk that you execute an innocent person.

Arguments 7 and 8 contradict each other, but both are evidence-based, i.e. they must be justified on the basis of evidence.

So here we have four ways in which our twenty-one propositions can be grouped. In each case, the criteria for and the objective of the grouping are different. In the first example, we might simply wish to assess the number and validity of arguments for and against capital punishment. In the second example, we might well wish to emphasise the superiority of the arguments based on evidence compared with arguments based on emotion or other drivers. In the third case, we might be attempting to expose the extent to which emotional/irrational arguments confuse the issue. In the fourth case, we might be trying to identify the different constituencies that participate in the argument with a view to presenting arguments to each of the groups that would be most likely to persuade them to our point of view.

In other words, our purpose is an important factor in determining how we group. Whether we realise it or not, the act of grouping adds meaning to the data, and if we know what we are doing when we group, we can make sure it is *our meaning* that will be added.

Appendix C | Interest – friend and foe

Year	£s owing	Int %	Int. £	Cum. £ Int.	£s paid	Balance	Cum. £s paid	Paid off	Paid off cum.
REPAYMENT PLAN ONE									
1	100,000	3	3,000	3,000	4,800	98,200	4,800	1,800	1,800
2	98,200	3	2,946	5,946	4,800	96,346	9,600	1,854	3,654
3	96,346	3	2,890	8,836	4,800	94,436	14,400	1,910	5,564
4	94,436	3	2,833	11,669	4,800	92,469	19,200	1,967	7,531
5	92,469	3	2,774	14,444	4,800	90,444	24,000	2,026	9,556
6	90,444	3	2,713	17,157	4,800	88,357	28,800	2,087	11,643
7	88,357	3	2,651	19,808	4,800	86,208	33,600	2,149	13,792
8	86,208	3	2,586	22,394	4,800	83,994	38,400	2,214	16,006
9	83,994	3	2,520	24,914	4,800	81,714	43,200	2,280	18,286
10	81,714	3	2,451	27,365	4,800	79,365	48,000	2,349	20,635
11	79,365	3	2,381	29,746	4,800	76,946	52,800	2,419	23,054
12	76,946	3	2,308	32,054	4,800	74,454	57,600	2,492	25,546
13	74,454	3	2,234	34,288	4,800	71,888	62,400	2,566	28,112
14	71,888	3	2,157	36,445	4,800	69,245	67,200	2,643	30,755
15	69,245	3	2,077	38,522	4,800	66,522	72,000	2,723	33,478
16	66,522	3	1,996	40,518	4,800	63,718	76,800	2,804	36,282
17	63,718	3	1,912	42,429	4,800	60,829	81,600	2,888	39,171
18	60,829	3	1,825	44,254	4,800	57,854	86,400	2,975	42,146
19	57,854	3	1,736	45,990	4,800	54,790	91,200	3,064	45,210
20	54,790	3	1,644	47,633	4,800	51,633	96,000	3,156	48,367

					REPAYMENT PLAN TWO				
Year	£s owing	Int. %	Int. £	Cum. £ Int	£s paid	Balance	Cum. £s paid	Paid off	Paid off cum.
1	100,000	3	3,000	3,000	9,600	**93,400**	9,600	6,600	**6,600**
2	93,400	3	2,802	5,802	9,600	**86,602**	19,200	6,798	**13,398**
3	86,602	3	2,598	8,400	9,600	**79,600**	28,800	7,002	**20,400**
4	79,600	3	2,388	10,788	9,600	**72,388**	38,400	7,212	**27,612**
5	72,388	3	2,172	12,960	9,600	**64,960**	48,000	7,428	**35,040**
6	64,960	3	1,949	14,908	9,600	**57,308**	57,600	7,651	**42,692**
7	57,308	3	1,719	16,628	9,600	**49,428**	67,200	7,881	**50,572**
8	49,428	3	1,483	18,111	9,600	**41,311**	76,800	8,117	**58,689**
9	41,311	3	1,239	19,350	9,600	**32,950**	86,400	8,361	**67,050**
10	32,950	3	988	20,338	9,600	**24,338**	96,000	8,612	**75,662**
11	24,338	3	730	21,069	9,600	**15,469**	105,600	8,870	**84,531**
12	15,469	3	464	21,533	9,600	**6,333**	115,200	9,136	**93,667**
13	6,333	3	190	21,723	9,600	**-3,077**	124,800	9,410	**103,077**